Esther P. Y. Tang
Ricky Y. K. Chan
Susan H. C. Tai
Editors

Asian Dimensions of Services Marketing

Asian Dimensions of Services Marketing has been co-published simultaneously as *Journal of International Consumer Marketing*, Volume 14, Number 1 2001.

Pre-publication REVIEWS, COMMENTARIES, EVALUATIONS . . .

"INSIGHTFUL . . . I AM PLEASED TO RECOMMEND IT. . . . It provides a bridge to the Asian psyche and how business is conducted in Asia. Practical examples are drawn from Singapore, Thailand, Korea, and China, with an integrative paper on country-of-origin effects."

E. Alan Buttery, PhD, MSc, FCIM FAIM, MAIM
Professor of Marketing
University of Western Sydney
Australia

More pre-publication
REVIEWS, COMMENTARIES, EVALUATIONS . . .

"**G**ives readers valuable insights on how Asian consumers think and behave and how they are different from Western consumers. . . . COULD BE USED AS A SUPPLEMENTARY READING BOOK FOR A SERVICE MARKETING COURSE."

Samart Powpaka, PhD
Associate Professor
Department of Marketing
The Chinese University
of Hong Kong

"**P**ROVIDES INSIGHTFUL EMPIRICAL STUDIES on targeting Asian consumers in at least four markets: China, Thailand, Korea, and Singapore. This book will be a welcome complement to any text on consumer behavior or services marketing."

Violeta A. Llanes, DBA
Senior Lecturer
Department of Marketing
School of Business
University of Otago, New Zealand

"**P**ACKED WITH RECOMMENDATIONS FOR MANAGERS AND ACADEMIC RESEARCHERS. . . . Examines very interesting topics, including country-of-origin perceptions, the emotional effects of environmental cues, and the relationship between social visibility, service exclusivity, and perceived risk."

Frank Bradley, PhD
R & A Bailey Professor
of International Marketing
Michael Smurfit Graduate School
of Business
University College, Dublin, Ireland

"**W**ELL WRITTEN. With rigorous methodology and insightful analysis, this volume illustrates the essence of Asian consumer behavior. INVALUABLE FOR PRACTICING MANAGERS AS WELL AS STUDENTS OF MARKETING."

Leo Sin, PhD
Professor, Department of Marketing
The Chinese University of Hong Kong

International Business Press
An Imprint of The Haworth Press, Inc.

Asian Dimensions
of Services Marketing

Asian Dimensions of Services Marketing has been co-published simultaneously as *Journal of International Consumer Marketing*, Volume 14, Number 1 2001.

The *Journal of International Consumer Marketing* Monographic "Separates"

Below is a list of "separates," which in serials librarianship means a special issue simultaneously published as a special journal issue or double-issue *and* as a "separate" hardbound monograph. (This is a format which we also call a "DocuSerial.")

"Separates" are published because specialized libraries or professionals may wish to purchase a specific thematic issue by itself in a format which can be separately cataloged and shelved, as opposed to purchasing the journal on an on-going basis. Faculty members may also more easily consider a "separate" for classroom adoption.

"Separates" are carefully classified separately with the major book jobbers so that the journal tie-in can be noted on new book order slips to avoid duplicate purchasing.

You may wish to visit Haworth's Website at . . .

http://www.HaworthPress.com

. . . to search our online catalog for complete tables of contents of these separates and related publications.

You may also call 1-800-HAWORTH (outside US/Canada: 607-722-5857), or Fax 1-800-895-0582 (outside US/Canada: 607-771-0012), or e-mail at:

getinfo@haworthpressinc.com

Asian Dimensions of Services Marketing, edited by Esther P. Y. Tang, Ricky Y. K. Chan, and Susan H. C. Tai (Vol. 14, No. 1, 2001). *Explores the trends of service industry from a variety of aspects in Asian countries such as Korea, Thailand, Singapore, and China.*

Consumer Behavior in Asia: Issues and Marketing Practice, edited by T. S. Chan, DBA (Vol. 11, No. 1, 1999). *Covers several important aspects of these behavior issues, including consumer attitudes and perceptions, market segmentation consideration, marketing communication, and influences of cultural forces.*

Global Perspectives in Cross-Cultural and Cross-National Consumer Research, edited by Lalita A. Manrai, PhD, and Ajay K. Manrai, PhD (Vol. 8, No. 3/4, 1996). *"A thought-provoking collection of chapters by some of the leading academics in the field of international marketing . . . A useful resource."* (What's New in Advertising & Marketing)

Global Tourist Behavior, edited by Muzaffer Uysal, PhD (Vol. 6, No. 3/4, 1994). *"Could prove very helpful to agents who want to get a better grip on what makes travelers tick."* (TRAVEL Counselor Magazine)

Asian Dimensions
of Services Marketing

Esther P. Y. Tang
Ricky Y. K. Chan
Susan H. C. Tai
Editors

Asian Dimensions of Services Marketing has been co-published simultaneously as *Journal of International Consumer Marketing*, Volume 14, Number 1 2001.

Routledge
Taylor & Francis Group

LONDON AND NEW YORK

First published 2018 by The Haworth Press, Inc.

2 Park Square, Milton Park, Abingdon, Oxfordshire OX14 4RN
605 Third Avenue, New York, NY 10017

Routledge is an imprint of the Taylor & Francis Group, an informa business

First issued in hardback 2020

Asian Dimensions of Services Marketing has been co-published simultaneously as *Journal of International Consumer Marketing*, Volume 14, Number 1 2001.

Cover design by Thomas J. Mayshock Jr.

Library of Congress Cataloging-in-Publication Data

Asian dimensions of services marketing / Esther P.Y. Tang, Ricky Y.K. Chan, Susan H.C. Tai, editors.
     p. cm.
   "Asian dimensions of services marketing has been co-published simultaneously as Journal of international consumer marketing, volume 14, number 1, 2001."
   Includes bibliographical references and index.
   ISBN 0-7890-1690-7 (hard : alk. paper)–ISBN 0-7890-1691-5 (pbk. alk. paper)
   1. Service industries–Asia–Marketing. 2. Consumers–Asia–Attitudes. I. Tang, Esther P. Y.
II. Chan, Ricky Y. K. III. Tai, Susan H. C. IV. Journal of international consumer marketing.

HD9987.A2 A85 2002
380.1945900095–dc21   2002017160

ISBN 978-0-7890-1690-4 (hbk)
ISBN 978-0-7890-1691-1 (pbk)

Indexing, Abstracting & Website/Internet Coverage

This section provides you with a list of major indexing & abstracting services. That is to say, each service began covering this periodical during the year noted in the right column. Most Websites which are listed below have indicated that they will either post, disseminate, compile, archive, cite or alert their own Website users with research-based content from this work. (This list is as current as the copyright date of this publication.)

(continued)

Special Bibliographic Notes related to special journal issues (separates) and indexing/abstracting:

- indexing/abstracting services in this list will also cover material in any "separate" that is co-published simultaneously with Haworth's special thematic journal issue or DocuSerial. Indexing/abstracting usually covers material at the article/chapter level.
- monographic co-editions are intended for either non-subscribers or libraries which intend to purchase a second copy for their circulating collections.
- monographic co-editions are reported to all jobbers/wholesalers/approval plans. The source journal is listed as the "series" to assist the prevention of duplicate purchasing in the same manner utilized for books-in-series.
- to facilitate user/access services all indexing/abstracting services are encouraged to utilize the co-indexing entry note indicated at the bottom of the first page of each article/chapter/contribution.
- this is intended to assist a library user of any reference tool (whether print, electronic, online, or CD-ROM) to locate the monographic version if the library has purchased this version but not a subscription to the source journal.
- individual articles/chapters in any Haworth publication are also available through the Haworth Document Delivery Service (HDDS).

Asian Dimensions of Services Marketing

CONTENTS

ABOUT THE EDITORS

Esther P. Y. Tang is Associate Professor in the Department of Business Studies at the Hong Kong Polytechnic University. She has conducted numerous marketing research projects within the commercial and industrial sectors. Her research interests focus on the interface of manufacturing and marketing, consumer variety-seeking behavior and the environmental impacts of business activities. Her research has been published in reputable international journals and presented at conferences.

Ricky Y. K. Chan is Associate Professor in the Department of Business Studies at the Hong Kong Polytechnic University. His research interests focus on behavioral issues of Chinese consumers and the operations of multinational corporations. He has contributed to such journals as *Business Horizons, International Business Review, Journal of Business Ethics, Journal of International Consumer Marketing, Journal of International Marketing, Journal of Services Marketing* and *Psychology and Marketing.*

Susan H. C. Tai is Assistant Professor in the Department of Business Studies at the Hong Kong Polytechnic University. Her current research focuses on success factors for advertising in China, the effects of store atmosphere on in-store shopping behavior, and the personal values of Chinese consumers. She has published in journals such as *Journal of International Consumer Marketing, Psychology and Marketing, International Journal of Advertising, Journal of Services Marketing* and *International Marketing Review.*

Foreword

As the Guest Co-Editors succinctly indicated in their "call for papers," The *Journal of International Consumer Marketing* is a leading forum for the dissemination of consumer/buyer behavior knowledge and experience on an international scale. It is designed to satisfy the current information needs of practicing global managers and public policy makers, as well as providing fresh ideas, concepts and techniques for classroom teachers and seasoned researchers of cross-cultural/national consumer behavior. With this in mind, this volume is devoted to the "Asian Dimensions of Services Marketing" which aims at providing the state-of-art knowledge in services marketing research and practice within the tertiary industry in the Asian region.

Customer satisfaction is the state of mind all marketing managers in the service and consumer goods categories strive for. There is a large body of research, both academic and commercial, that tells us a satisfied customer is one who is likely to be more loyal to his or her service provider/regular brand than a partially or dissatisfied customer. Furthermore, we know from experience that a loyal customer is a very valuable asset for several reasons: (a) a service or brand with the highest number of loyal customers is likely to be the market share leader; (b) loyal customers generally consume more of their regular service or brand than the less loyal customers and (c) it is almost always less expensive for a service provider/brand owner to retain a loyal customer than to acquire a new one.

It has been noted by marketing authorities that for some time now customer satisfaction research has been pre-eminent among US marketing researchers and practitioners; accounting for about one-third of the commercial research pie. While post-purchase goods and services satisfaction studies are "king" (Oliver 1999) in the US, and increasingly so in other Western countries, relatively little has been conducted in Southeast Asia.

The study by Patterson et al. examines the relationship between four service providers (medical, auto servicing, hairdressing and retail banking) and their

[Haworth co-indexing entry note]: "Foreword." Kaynak, Erdener. Co-published simultaneously in *Journal of International Consumer Marketing* (International Business Press, an imprint of The Haworth Press, Inc.) Vol. 14, No. 1, 2001, pp. xix-xxii; and: *Asian Dimensions of Services Marketing* (ed: Esther P. Y. Tang, Ricky Y. K. Chan, and Susan H. C. Tai) International Business Press, an imprint of The Haworth Press, Inc., 2001, pp. xi-xiv. Single or multiple copies of this article are available for a fee from The Haworth Document Delivery Service [1-800-342-9678, 9:00 a.m. - 5:00 p.m. (EST). E-mail address: getinfo@haworthpressinc.com].

xi

service delivery quality which includes a comfortable and friendly relationship as well as extra things the service provider might offer such as special gifts of bonuses. Another way of putting this is "going the extra mile" for the customer. However, it is a truism but nonetheless true that any service firm must deliver technical service with consistency if it wishes to stay in business.

The relationship of good or poor service performance with high or low customer satisfaction is clear enough until we introduce the idea that some services can not easily be judged by customers for their quality (medical and auto) while others easily can (hairdressing and retail banking). This relationship between the quality and level of service performance and customer satisfaction is further complicated by what we call switching costs or switching barriers. These switching costs are fairly new to marketing but extremely important in understanding the customer satisfaction/loyalty effect. We define switching costs as any barrier of an economic or psychological nature, which makes it difficult to change service providers. In our study we use high and low switching costs as moderators to tell us what happens to the relationship between service quality and satisfaction when they are in play.

The results of our research in very general terms show that switching costs have a very strong effect on the relationship between service performance and customer satisfaction across all four service providers. This means that when strong social bonds have been established with a service provider in Thailand the quality of the delivered service can drop without the customer's satisfaction level being negatively affected.

The lesson from our research is that firms or their managers must develop strong social ties with their customers right from the first service encounter, continue to provide the best service that they possibly can, yet be secure in the knowledge that there is a cushion called a switching cost if things go unexpectedly wrong, in the short run at least. This knowledge should be of particular interest to the giant Western retail chains that have come to Thailand in the last 3-4 years with their hundreds of expatriate staff and thereby changing retail patterns in major cities.

Along with increased level of socio-economic and technological development, the role of service industries is also rapidly increasing. The purpose of the study by Raymond and Mittelstaedt is to examine performance and operations of multinational service firms in Korea. In particular, the study explores perceived factors that both drive and inhibit success of multinational professional services firms in Korea. As well, the study investigates how these service firms position themselves with regard to various service attributes. Study results indicated that professional services MNCs operating in Korea ought to focus on internal (backstage) rather than external (front stage) activities. The absence of a service tradition in Korean culture requires that foreign services providers create a service culture within the context of Korean collectivism.

While managers may standardize some aspects of services in international markets, the aspects to be standardized may be different from market to market, based on the operating environment.

Reference group influence has been known to be an important determinant of an individual's behavior. The study by Mehta et al. was conducted to ascertain the importance of the different types of reference group influence on four categories of services differing in "conspicuousness" and importance (necessity versus luxury). In addition, the dominant perceived risk was ascertained for the different services. Data were collected from working women in Singapore, who, due to their affluence, are the focus of marketers in the region. Studies have indicated that working women are increasingly having a greater influence in all types of decisions within and outside the household. Results indicated that informational reference group influence has the most influential impact on all the decision to buy all the four services discussed, more so for luxury services. Utilitarian influence was also found to considerably affect consumer's choice of luxury services as well as services which are highly socially visible, whereas value expressive reference group influence was found to be high for publicly consumed services. For luxury services, financial and psychological risk were considered important. The authors provide a number of useful managerially oriented suggestions on promotional strategy for marketers of restaurants, beauty care services, haircut, and dental care services.

The study by Tang et al. empirically examines the emotional influence of environmental cues on Chinese consumers under a selected leisure service setting, a game center. Two important managerial implications have been derived from the present findings. First, on the affective side, the empirical results suggest that if game center visitors perceive the physical environment of the center as more positive, they will spend more time and money in it. Second, on the cognitive side, the results also indicate that game center visitor's perception of the physical environment of the center will positively affect their re-patronage intention in future. These implications help remind game center operators of the importance of store atmospherics to improve their current as well as future business performance. In view of this, these leisure service providers are advised to make every effort to ensure that the ambience, design, and layout match, as closely as possible, the tastes and preferences of their target customers. In addition to paying close attention to all aspects of the service environment during the design stages, these providers should continually track the possible changes of their customer's perceptions and re-patronage intention to ensure corporate success.

The research by Moon and Jain examines the impacts of consumer's two cross-national individual difference variables–country-of-origin perception and consumer ethnocentrism–on their responses and attitudes toward foreign advertisements. Empirical analysis of the hypothetical model through structural equation modeling yields supportive results: negative effects of consumer's ethnocentrism on their responses to the creative presentation of international advertising, and positive effects of consumer's country-of-origin perceptions on their responses to they buying proposal of international advertising.

Their study may contribute to our understanding of cross-national individual difference variables that precede and determine consumer's attitudes toward international advertising. It also has practical implications for the standardization versus localization debate in international advertising strategy. This study suggests some guidelines to determine the components and degree of localization of international advertising. It provides answers to the following questions: What elements of international advertising should be localized to appeal to foreign consumers? For which countries' target consumers should international ads be localized or standardized? If target market consumer's country-of-origin images of a product were weak, would it be strategically desirable to adapt a product and its advertising so that it could be promoted as different from, rather than typical of, that country's products?

Drs. Tang, Chan, and Tai are to be congratulated for bringing this insightful volume to a fruition. I am in the firm belief that the volume will contribute immensely to this under researched area of inquiry for many years to come. Happy reading!

Erdener Kaynak

Preface

One of the major developments that has taken place in Asia throughout the past few decades is the phenomenal growth of the service industry. As revealed by the relevant GDP figures, the service sector in many Asian countries is expanding at the expense of agriculture and manufacturing, and this mega-trend is expected to continue in the 21st century and beyond. The rapid development of services in Asia has resulted in a growing interest in special problems concerning how to effectively market intangibles of various kinds to consumers within the region. This leads to the launch of this special volume focusing on marketing services in Asia. The articles included in this collection cover several important aspects such as the influence of reference group in the service industry of Singapore, the moderating effect of switching costs on the relationship between service performance and customer satisfaction under a Thai cultural and business setting, perceived success factors for multinational professional services firms in (South) Korea, and the emotional impact of store atmospherics on Chinese customers in a leisure service setting.

The study by Mehta, Lalwani and Ping is aimed at investigating how reference group influences consumer behavior of Singaporean working women in four selected service categories differing in conspicuousness and importance (necessity versus luxury). Their results indicate that informational reference group influence has the most significant impact on all the four services, and more so for luxury services. These findings suggest that service marketers should focus on informational reference group to maximize their communication effectiveness. They should try their best to generate positive word of mouth, and pay heed to customer feedback and act promptly.

Specifically, their work suggests that service marketers should consider carefully the possibility of employing experts and professionals to influence their target customers. For instance, marketers of gourmet restaurants may invite connoisseurs to do a write-up in the relevant media to attract target diners.

[Haworth co-indexing entry note]: "Preface." Tang, Esther P.Y., Ricky Y.K. Chan, and Susan H.C. Tai. Co-published simultaneously in *Journal of International Consumer Marketing* (International Business Press, an imprint of The Haworth Press, Inc.) Vol. 14, No. 1, 2001, pp. xxiii-xxvi; and: *Asian Dimensions of Services Marketing* (ed: Esther P. Y. Tang, Ricky Y. K. Chan, and Susan H. C. Tai) International Business Press, an imprint of The Haworth Press, Inc., 2001, pp. xv-xviii. Single or multiple copies of this article are available for a fee from The Haworth Document Delivery Service [1-800-342-9678, 9:00 a.m. - 5:00 p.m. (EST). E-mail address: getinfo@haworthpressinc.com].

In short, it is believed that messages that focus on knowledge, expertise and credibility are essential for developing favorable customer attitudes toward the service offering. In addition to informational reference group influence, their study has identified utilitarian influence as another significant factor that strongly affects consumer's choice of luxury services as well as services whose results are highly socially visible. The findings help remind service marketers of the importance of social pressure or subjective norm in shaping the consumer selection process for these services.

The study conducted by Moon and Jain examines the impacts of consumer's two cross-national individual difference variables, namely country-of-origin perception and consumer ethnocentrism, on their responses and attitudes toward foreign advertisement. Their empirical analysis of the hypothetical model through structural equation modeling provides a number of supportive results. In particular, their results show that consumer's ethnocentrism exerts a negative influence on the responses to the creative presentation of international advertising, and their country-of-origin perceptions exhibit a positive impact on their responses to the buying proposal of international advertising.

These findings help provide further insights into understanding the standardization versus localization debate in international advertising. Specifically, these empirical results provide some practical guidelines to determine the components and degree of localization of international advertising. They help remind international marketing managers of the importance to clearly research the target customer's degree of consumer ethnocentrism and perception of country of origin alongside the characteristics of the advertised product in question.

Maximizing customer satisfaction is one of the major objectives that marketing managers in the service and consumer product categories often strive for. Moreover, it is universally agreed that a loyal customer is a very valuable asset for marketers in general and services providers in particular. Against this backdrop, Patterson, Mandhachitara "A" and Smith have examined the relationship between four selected service categories (medical service, auto servicing, hairdressing and retail banking) and their respective service delivery quality by administering a survey on 155 Thai consumers.

Consistent with the Western literature, their empirical work, by and large, indicates that satisfaction is the most important outcome of service encounters under a Thai cultural and business setting. Specifically, these researchers have demonstrated that technical and functional performance of the service provider exerts approximately equal explanatory power in shaping customer satisfaction. Despite the identified positive relationship between the quality of service performance and customer satisfaction, their study suggests that such a relationship is nevertheless moderated by switching costs or switching barriers. The finding implies that when strong social bonds have been established with a service provider in Thailand, the quality of the delivered service can drop without the customer's satisfaction level being negatively affected. The lesson derived from this research is that service providers operating in Thailand must develop strong social ties with their customers right from the first service encounter, continue to provide the best service that they possibly can, yet be secure in the knowledge that there is a cushion called switching costs if things go unexpectedly wrong. This knowledge should be of particular interest to those giant Western retail chains that started their business operations in Thailand in the last three to four years.

The investigation by Raymond and Mittelstaedt is aimed to explore perceptions of the factors that both drive and inhibit success of multinational professional services in Korea. The results of this investigation indicate that professional service multinational corporations in the country focus first on internal (back stage) activities such as service design, rather than external (front stage) activities such as meeting customer needs. This suggests that these corporations place a strong emphasis on organizational needs, which may be easier to standardize and many of which may be determined in their home country. Following that emphasis, they then focus on customer needs, which are likely to vary according to situations of the host country and thus require strategic adaptation.

As it is expected that more and more multinational service providers will enter the increasingly lucrative Korean market, the results of this study provide many practical insights for foreign investors and particularly multinational professional service firms. Most critical among these implications are those related to adapting strategies in order to operate successfully in the face of many uncontrollable factors and unique challenges of doing business in Korea. For instance, it is foreseen that the limited availability of work visas will continue to affect professional service providers. Coupled with the lack of a service attitude and highly skilled employees in Korea, foreign service providers thus need to carefully work out their human resources strategies for recruiting and training Korean nationals, and turn them into competent contact personnel.

Moreover, as image and reputation are of paramount importance in the Korean culture, it is essential for multinational service providers to establish relationship networks within the Korean community. This may involve recruiting employees from highly regarded Korean colleges and universities in order to establish a relationship with other alumni, which in turn would lead to more business. In addition, the findings from this study point to the importance of improving communication between clients and the service provider as well as within the service firm. In a collectivist community such as Korea, effective communication outside and within the service firm is regarded as absolutely essential to gain customer acceptance and to create a sense of belonging among employees.

The study by Tang, Chan and Tai empirically examines the emotional influence of environmental cues on Chinese consumers under a selected leisure service setting, namely a game center. To summarize, two important managerial implications have been derived from their work. First, on the affective side, their findings suggest that if game center visitors perceive the physical environment of the center as more positive, they will spend more time and money in it. Second, on the cognitive side, their analyses also indicate that game center visitor's perception of the physical environment of the center will positively affect their repatronage intention in future. These implications help remind game center operators of the importance of store atmospherics to improve their current as well as future business performance. In any event, it is advisable that leisure center operators should make every effort to ensure that the ambience, design, and layout of their center match, as closely as possible, the tastes and preferences of their target customers. In addition to paying close attention to all aspects of the service environment during the design stages, they should continually track the possible changes of their customer's perceptions and repatronage intention to ensure corporate success.

Esther P.Y. Tang
Ricky Y.K. Chan
Susan H.C. Tai

Switching Costs as a Moderator of Service Satisfaction Processes in Thailand

Paul G. Patterson
Rujirutana Mandhachitara "A"
Tasman Smith

SUMMARY. Satisfaction is a well established outcome of a successful service encounter, and increasingly satisfaction is being linked to perhaps the most important construct in marketing–behavioral loyalty. In this paper satisfaction as the dependent variable is regressed on technical quality and functional quality, as independent variables. However, the study moves beyond the modeling the pure antecedents of satisfaction to a contingency model of satisfaction evaluation where psychological switching costs is employed as a moderator. The results show that switching costs have a strong impact on the relationship between technical and functional quality, and satisfaction, across all four service indus-

---

Paul G. Patterson is Professor, School of Marketing, University of New South Wales, Sydney 2052, Australia (E-mail: p.patterson@unsw.edu.au). Rujirutana Mandhachitara "A" is a doctoral student in marketing, Thammasat Business School, Thammasat University, 2 Prachan Road, Bangkok 10200 Thailand (E-mail: ruji@alpha.tu.ac.th). Tasman Smith is Professor and Chairman, Graduate Marketing Studies, Thammasat Business School, Thammasat University, 2 Prachan Road, Bangkok 10200 Thailand (E-mail: tsmith@alpha.tu.ac.th).

The authors would like to thank the two anonymous reviewers whose contributions have certainly made this a better paper. Reviewer B, in particular, demonstrated a diligence and commitment which was greatly appreciated by and helpful to the authors.

[Haworth co-indexing entry note]: "Switching Costs as a Moderator of Service Satisfaction Processes in Thailand." Patterson, Paul G., Rujirutana Mandhachitara "A", and Tasman Smith. Co-published simultaneously in *Journal of International Consumer Marketing* (International Business Press, an imprint of The Haworth Press, Inc.) Vol. 14, No. 1, 2001, pp. 1-21; and: *Asian Dimensions of Services Marketing* (ed: Esther P. Y. Tang, Ricky Y. K. Chan, and Susan H. C. Tai) International Business Press, an imprint of The Haworth Press, Inc., 2001, pp. 1-21. Single or multiple copies of this article are available for a fee from The Haworth Document Delivery Service [1-800-342-9678, 9:00 a.m. - 5:00 p.m. (EST). E-mail address: getinfo@haworthpressinc.com].

1

tries studied in Thailand. In other words, the impact of technical and functional quality varies under different contingency conditions. *[Article copies available for a fee from The Haworth Document Delivery Service: 1-800-342-9678. E-mail address: <getinfo@haworthpressinc.com> Website: <http://www.HaworthPress.com> © 2001 by The Haworth Press, Inc. All rights reserved.]*

KEYWORDS. Service satisfaction, switching costs, Thailand

INTRODUCTION

Satisfaction with services has been shown to be a function of both technical and functional performance (Gronroos, 1995; Yi, 1993). However, the relative impact of technical performance and functional performance on satisfaction may be different across a range of services (Kasper et al., 1999). One case of this is the distinction which has been made in the literature between services that are high in credence or experience properties (Zeithaml, 1981; Darby and Karni, 1973). Credence properties are associated with difficulty in assessing the quality of the service provided while services with high experience qualities are sufficiently uncomplicated that the customer can form an opinion of its quality immediately. The differential impact of technical performance and functional performance on satisfaction in different types of services may be caused by different levels of switching costs (Jackson, 1985; Anderson, 1994; Maute and Forrester, 1993). Hence, the objective of this study then is to empirically test the moderating effect of switching costs on the relationships between technical and functional performance, and customer satisfaction in services characterized by having high credence and experience properties.

Service Satisfaction

Satisfaction is the post-purchase evaluation of a service following a consumption experience. It is thought to posses both cognitive and affective components (Bitner, 1990; Oliver and Swan, 1989). Satisfaction in this study refers to the overall experience of a customer during the process of receiving a service from the provider. Cronin and Taylor (1992), Patterson et al. (1997) and Oliver and Swan (1989) found that consumer satisfaction has a significant impact on repurchase intention in a range of services. Crosby et al. (1990) also suggests that future sales opportunities depend directly on trust and satisfaction in personal selling situations, while Day et al. (1988) conclude that customer satisfaction is unquestionably the key determinant in retaining customers in services.

Hence this study strengthens the satisfaction/dissatisfaction paradigm, forthwith referred to as CSD, literature as a dependent variable with the inclusion of two antecedents, technical and functional performance. Furthermore the impact of the moderator variable (switching costs) is hypothesized to vary across service types (credence versus experience). Therefore the study will help answer the question: When does a particular antecedent (technical or functional performance) have a weaker/stronger impact on of satisfaction? This is a shift is from the "Is" question to the "When" question (Yi, 1993). Figure 1 refers.

For many services, the service delivery process or how the service is delivered, often takes on equal importance to what is delivered. Therefore a distinction should be drawn between technical and functional performance (Gronroos, 1995). Technical performance refers to delivery of the core service (what the customer is buying), while functional performance is the customer's perception of the service delivery process (how the service is delivered). In the service quality literature, functional performance is equivalent to the SERVQUAL dimensions of assurance, empathy and responsiveness, while technical performance equates more to the reliability dimension (Parasuraman, Zeithaml and Berry, 1988; Patterson and Smith, 2001).

Several studies have successfully modeled CSD as a function of performance attributes alone, rather than performance versus expectations or the disconfirmation paradigm (Cronin and Taylor, 1992; Patterson and Johnson, 1995; de Ruyter et al. 1997). There seems to be a gap in the literature which ex-

FIGURE 1. Conceptual Model

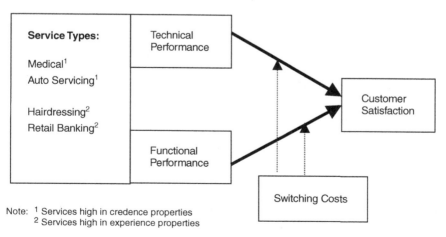

Note: [1] Services high in credence properties
[2] Services high in experience properties

amines the moderating impact of psychological switching costs on the satisfaction model, when CSD is conjectured as a direct function of technical and functional performance.

It would seem likely that the impact of switching costs as a moderator might vary depending on whether the service is high in credence or experience properties. Credence properties refer to those services where the customer typically has difficulty evaluating the quality of what they have received (due to lack of specialist technical expertise) either during or even following consumption (Zeithaml, 1981; Darby and Karni 1973). For example, most customers are likely to have difficulty evaluating whether the medical advice they received is appropriate, or whether their automobile was in fact serviced in the most expeditious manner by their mechanic. Services high in experience properties on the other hand, can be evaluated for quality and value immediately following the consumption experience, e.g., a vacation, hairdressing, movie, sporting event).

Oliver (1999) for example notes that for some time now satisfaction research has been pre-eminent among US marketing scholars and practitioners. Satisfaction research has become "king" he observes (Oliver, 1999). Oliver also refers to the large percentage of the commercial research pie (one-third) that is accounted for by satisfaction research (p. 33). Furthermore, this view is supported by Zeithaml and Bitner (1996) and Gilly and Graham (1996) who emphasize the established importance of post-purchase goods and services satisfaction studies in the United States. Still very little scholarly customer satisfaction research has been published concerning Southeast Asia (Malhotra et al., 1994; Winsted, 1999).

Modeling the process of customer satisfaction/dissatisfaction has been the subject of numerous conceptual and empirical works since Cardozo's (1965) study, with sometimes mixed and conflicting results. Satisfaction is a consumer's post-purchase evaluation and affective response to the overall product or service experience (Oliver, 1994). In the case of services, because the consumer is often in the "service factory," CSD is a function of both how the firm performs on the technical service dimension (a good haircut; the car is serviced properly the first time) and how the customer is treated during the service process or functional performance (personalized attention from the hairdresser or bank staff remembering your name).

The dominant conceptual model, the disconfirmation of expectations paradigm, posits that CSD is related to the size and direction of the disconfirmation experience, where disconfirmation is defined as the difference between a consumer's pre-purchase expectations (or some other comparison standard) and perceptions of post-purchase performance (Anderson, 1973; Churchill and Surprenant, 1982; Oliver, 1980; Zeitham, Berry and Parasuaman, 1996; Patterson, Johnson and Spreng, 1997; Tse and Wilton 1988). Others have successfully modeled CSD and service quality (a related but different construct) as a function of performance perceptions alone (e.g., Cronin and Taylor, 1992). CSD as a direct function of performance perceptions seems operationally quite manageable.

However, a fruitful and possibly more insightful way of capturing changes in service satisfaction would be to attempt to model the satisfaction process under different contingency conditions. This approach has not much been used with the exception of Yi (1993), Patterson and Johnson (1993), and Sharma and Patterson (1999) who found that product experience moderates the CSD formation process. An understanding of how switching costs moderates customer satisfaction processes would be helpful to scholars understand service satisfaction better and be of possible value to practitioners in building service businesses.

Technical and Functional Performance

It is almost a "given" that any service firm must deliver the core or technical service with consistency if it wishes to stay in business (Groonroos, 1983; Kasper et al. 1999). However customers seek and appreciate other benefits which relate to processes or how the service is delivered (referred to as functional quality, e.g., Gronroos, 1983). Such benefits include social motives which encompass the comfortable and friendly ambience that is built up in some service relationships, as well as the extra things that a service provider might do (an added or unsought bonus) for a long-term, loyal customer (Gwinner, Gremler and Bitner, 1998). Furthermore, the provision of relevant and timely information can in some services add value for a customer (e.g., informative tourist brochures, information on a particular medical condition or remedy).

Furthermore it would be valuable to examine the two types of performance described above, technical and functional (Gronroos, 1983), in relation to the degree of customer satisfaction across different service types. Sampling in four service industries would give the findings greater robustness than in just a single industry setting. We therefore propose examining four industries; medical and auto servicing, which are characterized by being high in credence properties, and hairdressing and retail banking, which are high in experience properties (Darby and Karni, 1973).

Switching Costs

Jones and Sasser (1995) observe that switching barriers has received relatively little attention in marketing and moreover that while customer satisfaction is usually the key element in securing repeat patronage, this outcome may be dependent on switching barriers arising in the context of service provision

(Jones et al., 2000). Similar suggestions have been made in support of switching costs by Anderson (1994). Switching costs, on the other hand, is conceptualized as the perception of the magnitude of the incremental costs required to terminate a relationship and secure an alternative (Porter, 1980). Switching or termination costs have been identified as a factor contributing to the continuation of long-term business relationships. Some scholars see switching costs in economic terms only (Morgan and Hunt, 1994). Jackson (1985), however, popularized switching costs in her study of industrial marketing relationships as being psychological, physical and economic in nature. In this study we conceive of switching costs as any barrier which makes it more difficult to change service providers (Jones and Sasser, 1995).

When considering a switch in suppliers, a customer faces a number of setup costs and takedown costs (Weiss and Anderson, 1992). Setup costs might include search effort, the emotional drain in establishing a new interpersonal relationship, and the perceived risk that a new supplier might not perform at a level of performance equal to, or better than, the current supplier. Takedown costs include relationship specific investments made by the customer that have no value outside the current relationship. In a consumer service setting, these costs relate mainly to the psychological costs of terminating a friendly and comfortable relationship; being recognized by service personnel; being treated as more than just another customer; and enjoying social aspects of the interpersonal interactions, e.g., client relationship with their doctors, banker, hairdressers or auto services mechanic. Hence some customers will be motivated to avoid the accompanying psychological and emotional stress that comes with terminating such quasi-social relationships.

The moderating effect of perceived high and low psychological switching costs on the relationship between performance and CSD is now considered. When a social relationship has been established with a service provider, i.e., psychological switching barriers have developed, then functional performance ("how" the customer is treated during service delivery) becomes central to generating customer satisfaction. This is especially the case for services high in credence properties where customers typically have great difficulty evaluating the technical quality of the service performance. In credence services, even though customers often have difficulty in confidently evaluating technical quality when social bonds have yet to be formed (low psychological switching costs), functional performance (how customers are treated during interpersonal service encounters) will have a lower impact on CSD evaluation compared to subjective assessments of technical performance. For experience services, on the other hand, customers can confidently evaluate technical quality. Hence even when social bonds have been formed (psychological switching costs), functional performance (how customers are treated during interpersonal service encounters) will have a lower impact of CSD evaluation compared to assessments of technical performance.

Hypotheses

In credence services, customers cannot evaluate the outcomes of using the service (technical performance). But they can and do evaluate how they are treated during the process of service delivery, especially when social bonds have been developed. Hence the impact of functional performance on satisfaction will be higher when switching cost is high than when switching cost is low (H1); and the impact of technical performance on satisfaction will be higher than that of functional performance on satisfaction when switching cost is low (H2).

For services high in experience properties, customers can confidently evaluate technical performance quality following the service experience. So the impact of functional performance on satisfaction will only be higher when switching cost is high (i.e., strong social bonds have been formed) than when switching cost is low (H3). However, under either low or high switching cost conditions, technical quality will have a greater impact on CSD than functional performance (H4).

RESEARCH METHODOLOGY

In phase one, ten qualitative interviews were conducted plus 25 personal diary descriptions gathered in Bangkok, Thailand across a range of services so as to gain an understanding of the Thai antecedents of customer satisfaction with a service provider. This was followed by a cross sectional survey (using a self-administered questionnaire) of four service industries. In line with Darby and Karni's (1973) classification (experience versus credence properties), this formed the basis for selecting the four service industries: medical, auto servicing, hairdressing and retail banking.

Respondents were recruited by graduate business students at a major university in Bangkok who gave a set of (4) self-administered questionnaires (in the Thai language) to family and friends. The original questionnaires were constructed in English, then translated and back translated by Thai personnel skilled in both English and Thai, as well as the marketing literature. The questionnaires were then pretested to ensure the English meaning of various concepts, phrases and even words were equivalent in the Thai language. Some modifications were necessary as some words or phrases had no comparable Thai equivalent. A total of 180 questionnaires sets were distributed. The final sample comprised 155 respondents who completed all questionnaires over a period of two weeks. Each respondent was asked to complete one questionnaire every two days so as to avoid order effects. Furthermore the order was randomised and instructions specified the order in which the questionnaires were to be completed. A quota sampling procedure was used (each student was given a profile of the respondents required). A good spread of age, sex and occupational profiles was achieved. A demographic profile of respondents is shown in the Appendix 1.

Scales

Scales for key constructs of customer satisfaction, functional and technical performance quality and switching costs were sourced from the extant literature, and modified where necessary based on results of qualitative interviews. The customer satisfaction scale was based on Oliver and Swan (1989), while the switching costs were derived from Ping (1993) and the items for the functional and technical performance were based on Gronroos (1983); Parasuraman and Berry (1988); Sharma and Patterson (1999). Hence the scales are considered to have construct validity. Face validity was achieved by showing the questionnaires to one service provider in each of the 4 industries and two academics familiar with the relationship literature. Minor modification to some question wording was necessary as a result. Samples of all scale items are shown in Appendix 2. All exhibited good internal reliability with Cronbach's alpha coefficients mostly above 0.80.

Moderator Subgroup Analysis

A moderator is a variable that effects the strength or direction (slope) of a relationship between an explanatory variable and a dependent variable (Baron and Kenny, 1986). Moderation of the form or nature of a relationship is detected by examining for interaction effects in the analysis of variance or significant differences in regression coefficients across sub-groups (Arnold, 1982).

The hypotheses tested in this study refer to the nature or form of the relationship. In order to examine the moderating effects of the contingency variables, a sub-group analysis (Arnold, 1982; Kohli, 1989) was performed. More specifically, ordinary least squares (OLS) regression analysis was repeated in sub-groups reflecting low and high scores on the moderator variable (psychological switching costs). In forming a pair of sub-groups representing "low" and "high" scores on the moderator variable, observations were first sorted into ascending order. Two sub-groups were then formed by selecting approximately the top and bottom 45% of observations (cases). The middle 10% were dropped from subsequent analysis so as to increase the contrast between the sub-groups. This contrast is evident in Table 1 which displays the mean and standard deviation for the two sub-groups. The Chow test (Chow, 1960) was then performed to establish the significance of the difference in the *form* (or slope) of the regression model across the high and low sub-groups. This is an omnibus test that assesses whether an overall difference exists in parameter values between groups, but does not assess the significance of the individual parameter estimate (Gunst and Mason, 1980). Significant differences in the individual regression coefficients for technical and functional performance were tested using unpaired t-tests. An important consideration is sub-group analysis is equivalence of variance across groups. The Levene test for heteroscedascity was run and established that population variance across sub-groups were equal.

Validity and Reliability of Measures

The four satisfaction items were sourced from Oliver and Swan (1989) and Patterson, Johnson and Spreng (1997), and are thus considered to have construct validity. Factor analysis (principal components with varimax rotation) confirmed the items to be unidimensional across the four service types. Cronbach's alpha (measure of reliability) ranged from 0.92 (auto servicing) to 0.94 (medical and retail banking). Thus the dependent variable was considered to have validity and reliability.

The performance items were subjected to an exploratory factor analysis (varimax rotation) and revealed two clean dimensions labeled technical performance and functional performance. Two items did not load cleanly (factor loading > 0.50 on one dimension alone) and were subsequently excluded from the performance measures in all service types. Otherwise the items loaded cleanly on the same factors in all four service types, indicating the robustness of the measures. Cronbach's alpha ranged from 0.85 (hairdressing–technical performance) to 0.95 (retail banking–functional performance). Appendix 2 refers. Factor analysis of the four item moderator variable, psychological switching costs, was revealed to be unidimensional and have Cronbach's alphas ranging from 0.77 (medical) to 0.80 (auto servicing). Finally, in order to examine if there was any confounding effect on satisfaction from demographic factors, differences in the performance variables between the high and low

TABLE 1. Descriptive Statistics for Moderator Variable (Switching Costs)

Service type	Low Sub-group			High Sub-group		
	n	Mean	St. Dev.	n	Mean	St. Dev
Medical	52	2.41	.56	87	4.05	.53
Auto Servicing	60	2.49	.66	77	4.02	.55
Hairdressing	70	2.60	.55	62	4.28	.48
Retail Banking	59	2.75	.51	73	3.87	.52

moderator groups (switching costs) for all four service industries were examined. We ran a one-way ANOVA for age and sex and found no statistically significant relationships in the average performance scores for each high and low subgroup. Referring to the correlation matrix for all four service categories studied (Table 2), it should be noted that switching costs has only modest correlations with both the independent and dependent variables, thus providing support for its role as a moderator variable.

RESULTS AND DISCUSSION

First, for the total sample it is worth noting from Table 3 that for all four service categories, technical performance is considerably more important in shaping satisfaction evaluations than functional performance (for example in medical services the unstandized regression coefficient (b) for Techperf is 0.56 versus only b = 0.19 for Functperf).

Next when analyzing the results according to high and low switching costs, it should be noted that the Chow test reveals that there are statistically significant differences in the form of the regression equations across sub-groups for all four service categories (F ranging from 5.46 to 43.9). In other words, as hypothesized switching costs does moderate the impact of technical and functional performance on satisfaction across all four service types. To validate the sub-group analysis, we also performed moderator regression. An interaction term was computed and moderator regression was also run for all four ser-

TABLE 2. Zero Order Correlations

Medical					Auto Servicing				
	1	2	3	4		1	2	3	4
1. Satisfaction	1.00				1. Satisfaction	1.00			
2.Techperf	.67	1.00			2.Techperf	.74	1.00		
3. Functperf	.54	.77	1.00		3. Functperf	.62	.68	1.00	
4. Switch cost	.23	.25	.23	1.00	4. Switch cost	.42	.42	.46	1.00
Hairdressing					Retail Banking				
	1	2	3	4		1	2	3	4
1. Satisfaction	1.00				1. Satisfaction	1.00			
2.Techperf	.64	1.00			2.Techperf	.73	1.00		
3. Functperf	.57	.63	1.00		3. Functperf	.66	.79	1.00	
4. Switch cost	.36	.33	.44	1.00	4. Switch cost	.32	.38	.37	1.00

Note: Techperf = Technical performance and Functperf = Functional performance

TABLE 3. Regression Results (Standardized)

	Medical				Auto Servicing				Hairdressing				Retail Banking			
	Techperf (b)	Functperf (b)	Adj R^2	Chow/test (F)	Techperf (b)	Functperf (b)	Adj R^2	Chow/test (F)	Techperf (b)	Functperf (b)	Adj R^2	Chow/test (F)	Techperf (b)	Functperf (b)	Adj R^2	Chow/test (F)
Total Sample (n = 155)	.561	.187	41.7%		.636	.202	52.3%		.400	.339	42.9%		.641	.255	57.5%	
Low Switch Costs	.757	.011	44.6%	39.7[a]	.814	.003	55.6%	43.9[a]	.270	.351	32.7%	5.46[b]	.622	.295	64.9%	21.2[a]
High Switch Costs	.261 (.001)	.430 (.001)	33.5%		.567 (.001)	.446 (.001)	56.2%		.396 (.01)	.379 (ns)	39.4%		.508 (.01)	.375 (.05)	50.4%	

Note: [a] $p < .001$
[b] $p < .01$
ns not significant at $p < .05$
Figures in brackets represents the significance of the t-test between raw regression coefficients, (b) for low and high sub-groups.
Techperf = Technical performance; Functperf = Functional performance

vices. With the interaction term included, the regression results should show a small (but significant) increase in R^2. In three of the four services this proved to be the case. This provides strong supporting evidence for the sub-group analysis results. However for the retail banking sample the increase in R^2 was less than one per cent. This probably reflects the fact that moderator regression treats the moderator as a continuous variable, whereas the sub-group analysis divides the sample into discrete high and low sub-groups (see Table 4).

We now report the results of individual hypotheses testing.

Hypothesis 1 stated that for credence services functional performance would have a stronger impact on CSD under conditions of high (rather than low) switching costs. Our data support this assertion with functional performance having standardized betas (β) of 0.40 (medical) and 0.39 (auto service) for the high switching cost sub-group versus only 0.09 and 0.07 respectively, ($p \leq 0.001$) for the low sub-groups. Hence H1 is fully supported.

Hypothesis H2 states that for credence services technical performance will have a greater impact than functional performance on CSD when switching costs are low. H2 asserted the opposite trend under high switching cost conditions. For medical and auto services the betas for technical performance were ($\beta = 0.74$ and 0.80 (low sub-groups) respectively versus only ($\beta = 0.09$ and 0.07 for functional performance. Differences are significant at $p \leq 0.001$. Hence H2 is fully supported.

The third hypotheses asserted that for the "experience" services, functional performance would have a stronger impact on CSD under high switching cost conditions. For retail banking services this was so with $\beta = 0.36$ (high sub-group) versus $\beta = 0.30$ (low sub-group). This difference is significant at $p \leq 0.05$. However, for the hairdressing services sample, the findings were reversed with $\beta = 0.30$ (high sub-group) and $\beta = 0.38$ (low sub-group) ($p \leq 0.05$). An explanation for this latter result might be that hairdressing, being a high-contact service (as the opposite to low-contact for retail banking), customers with perceived lower switching costs place greater value on good personal service. And furthermore, it may be that they are motivated to seek a stronger personal relationship with their individual hairdresser, and hence functional performance is stronger under low switching cost conditions.

It is also asserted that technical performance would have a greater impact under high switching cost conditions. For hairdressing services this was the case with $\beta = 0.42$ (high sub-group) versus $\beta = 0.27$ (low sub-group). However for retail banking the data depicts the reverse trend with $\beta = 0.41$ and 0.53 for high and low sub-groups, respectively. Hence H3 is only partially supported. It appears that retail banking customers perceive low psychological barriers to switching, therefore, they place greater importance on the technical merits of

TABLE 4. Regression Results (Standardized)

Standardized Parameter Estimates (β)

| | Credence Properties | | | | | | Experience Properties | | | | | |
| | Medical | | | Auto Servicing | | | Hairdressing | | | Retail Banking | | |
	Techperf (B)	Functperf (B)	Adj R²	Techperf (B)	Functperf (B)	Adj R²	Techperf (B)	Functperf (B)	Adj R²	Techperf (B)	Functperf (B)	Adj R²
Total Sample	.509	.178	41.7%	.567	.207	52.3%	.413	.315	42.9%	.535	.253	57.5%
Low Switch Costs	.742	.09	44.6%	.805	.07	55.8%	.273	.377	32.7%	.534	.301	64.9%
High Switch Costs	.228	.400	33.5%	.439	.393	56.2%	.423	.300	39.4%	.410	.361	50.4%

Note: Techperf = Technical performance
Functperf = Functional performance

13

the banks, performance in making their satisfaction/dissatisfaction evaluations. This is probably partly due to the fact that as banking is a low contact service it is difficult to forge interpersonal relationships (a key component of functional performance).

Hypothesis 4 stated that for services possessing experience properties, under both high and low switching conditions, technical performance would have a greater impact than functional performance on CSD. For retail banking services this proved to be the case (refer to Table 1). However for hairdressing services the data only supports the hypothesis in the high switching cost condition ($\beta = 0.42$ versus $\beta = 0.30$ for technical and functional respectively). Hence H4 is only partially supported. This may be due to the fact that under low switching cost conditions customers are less inhibited to switch, know exactly what technical performance should be, and thus place a higher value on the quasi-friendship relationship (functional performance) they develop with an individual hairdresser.

CONCLUSION

In the absence of any contingency conditions, technical and functional performance were shown to have approximately equal explanatory power in shaping customer satisfaction. The results of the study show that the moderator variable, psychological switching costs, has a major impact on the nature of the relationship between key antecedents (technical and functional quality) and the dependent variable, customer satisfaction, for both experience and credence type services. In effect, the findings mean we have several contingency models of satisfaction evaluation, each applicable under different conditions, thus indicating that future studies of satisfaction need to take into account the fact that the nature of the relationship between the antecedents and satisfaction are context specific. Hence in future we should consider other contingency (moderator variables) such as perceived product/service complexity, focal brand experience and level of personal involvement and examine whether these variables also have a moderator impact. For example, highly experienced customers may evaluate technical quality for more confidently than less experienced ones. Or under high (as opposed to low) personal involvement conditions, customers of both experience and credence services may spend more cognitive effort evaluating technical quality. In other words modeling the satisfaction evaluation process is far more complex than the hitherto macro models suggest.

Managerial Implications

This study makes no claim to be a cross-cultural one as it was conducted only in Thailand, yet the results tell us quite a lot about operating a service business in Thailand. Abramson and Ai (1998) draw our attention to the dangers of North Americans doing business in Southeast Asia when they posit that the latter area is much more relationship-oriented. In the same vein Malholtra et al. (1994) have warned that "it is important for international marketing managers to understand the various environmental, economic and social-cultural factors that effect consideration in service quality evaluation" (p. 14).

Within the limited scope of this paper it has not been possible to examine more than two antecedents and one moderator of service satisfaction. A strong case can be make for satisfaction as the most important outcome of service encounters globally. To wit, Winsted (1999) points out that very little scholarly satisfaction research has been published concerning Southeast Asia. Jean-Claude Usunier (1996) and others note that in Asia the preservation of social harmony is more highly valued than the indulgence of expressing dissatisfaction or exhibiting complaining behavior. Schutte and Ciarlante (1998) even go so far as to suggest that in a commercial relationship in Thailand "an act of direct criticism is regarded at best as a sign of bad manners, and at worst as a deliberate attempt to offend" (p. 114).

Our research does not support or reject these observations. However the importance of the moderator variable (switching costs) in mitigating the relationship between performance (technical and functional quality) for services high in both experience and credence qualities is consistent with the cultural observations made in the above first two paragraphs. Putting this a little differently, the marketing practitioner in Thailand can assume that when strong social bonds have been formed in a service relationship customers will be forgiving of core service failures and such lapses will have only a minor impact on customers overall satisfaction judgements. Hence local firms and international marketers from the West would be well advised to develop strong social ties with customers in the event of a less than superior core service performance. Finally, as a general caveat to services marketing manager, our results show that there is not one generalizable macro satisfaction process, but rather it will vary under different switching cost conditions.

Limitations of the Study

The principal limitation of this study is that it was conducted only in Thailand and as such cannot be viewed as cross-cultural. Because of this limitation we cannot draw on the rich research of Hofstede (1980), Triandis (1995) among others who have classified Thailand as a collectivist culture with many differences to the individualist cultures of the USA and Western Europe. This means we have had to minimize as far as practicable this cross-cultural literature.

Another weakness of the study is the relatively few (Jones, Motherbaugh and Beatty, 2000) other studies in the service marketing field that have been conducted using moderator variables. This makes comparison of results difficult and our ability to generalize findings from an adequate body of service literature impossible.

Also, the study perhaps included too few variables, notably of moderators such as service experience (Cadotte et al. 1987) and alternative attractiveness (Ping, 1993; Rusbultt, 1980; Sharma and Patterson, 2000). Similarly variables which have proved important in customer satisfaction research, such as equity (fairness), expectations (Patterson et al. 1999) and or commitment (Crosby et al. 1990; Cronin and Taylor, 1992; Patterson and Smith 2001) were not included in the study. Jones, Mothersbaugh and Beatty (2000) demonstrate the strong relationship between service satisfaction and customer retention which has also been earlier discussed by Maute and Forrester (1993) and Anderson (1994). This variable deserves inclusion because of the importance of customer retention in marketing (Fornell, 1992).

Finally, it would have been helpful to track some of the consequences of service satisfaction, such as word of month recommendation, resistance to counter-persuasion and level of variety seeking behavior (Dick and Basu, 1994).

Future Research Directions

The logical next step to this paper would be a cross-cultural study conducted in Bangkok and perhaps an American city of a similar size. A well-specified conceptual model might include technical and functional performance as mediators; switching costs, alternative attractiveness, previous service experience, demographic and selected cultural factors as moderators; service satisfaction as the dependent variable; with the consequences set as trust commitment, word of month recommendation, resistance to counter-persuasion and variety seeking behavior. In order to ensure sufficient power (Cohen, 1988) a sample of approximately 500 respondents would be required in each city. Rather than ordinary least squares regression analysis we would employ structural equations modeling to permit a more insightful analysis of the larger database and the increased number of variables. Such a study would serve to answer many of the questions posed by the results reported in this paper and for which a cross-cultural interpretation is tempting but not justified.

REFERENCES

Abramson, Neil and Janet X. Ai. (1998). Practicing Relationship Marketing in Southeast Asia: Reducing Uncertainty and Improving Performance, *Management International Review*, Annual, 38 (31), 113-147.

Andersen, Eugene W. (1994). Cross-Category Variation in Customer Satisfaction and Retention, *Marketing Letters*, 5 (1): 19-30.

Anderson, R.E. (1973). Consumer Dissatisfaction: The Effect of Disconfirmed Expectancy on Perceived Product Performance, *Journal of Consumer Research*, 10 (February), 38-44.

Arnold, H.J. (1982). Moderator Variables: A Classification of Conceptual, Analytical and Psychometric Issues, *Organizational Behaviour and Human Performance*, 29, 143-174.

Baron, R.M. and D.A. Kenny. (1986). The Moderator-Mediator Variable Distinction in Social Psychological Research: Conceptual, Strategic and Statistical Considerations, *Journal of Personality and Social Psychology*, 51 (6), 1173-1182.

Bitner, M.J. (1990). Evaluating service encounters: the effects of physical surroundings and employee response, *Journal of Marketing*, 54 (April), 69-82.

Cadotte, E.E.; Woodruss, R.B. and Jenkins, R.L. (1987). Expectations and norms in models of consumer satisfaction, *Journal of Marketing Research*, 24 (August), 305-314.

Cardozo, R.N. (1965). An Experimental Study of Consumer Effort, Expectations and Satisfaction, *Journal of Consumer Research*, 2 (August), 244-249.

Chow, G.C. (1960).Test of equality between sets of coefficients in two linear regressions, *Econometrica*, 28 (July), 591-605.

Churchill, G.A. and C. Surprenant. (1982). An Investigation into the Determinants of Customer Satisfaction, *Journal of Marketing Research*, 19 (November), 491-504.

Cohen, Jacob C. (1988). *Statistical Power Analysis for the Behavioral Services (Second Edition)*, New Jersey: Lawrence Erlbaum.

Cronin, J.J. and Stephen A. Taylor. (1992). Measuring Service Quality, A Reexamination and Extension, *Journal of Marketing*, 56 (July), 55-68.

Crosby, L.A.; Evans, K.R. and Cowles, D. (1990), Relationship quality in services selling: an interpersonal influence perspective, *Journal of Marketing*, 54 (July), 68-81.

Darby, M.R. and E.R. Karni. (1973). Free Competition and Optimal Amount of Fraud, *Journal of Law and Economics*, 16 (April), 67-86.

Day, E.; Denton, L.L. and Hickner, J.A. (1998). Client's selection and retention criteria: some marketing implications for the small CPA firm, *Journal of Professional Services Marketing*, 3 (4), 85-91.

de Ruyter, Ko; Jose Bloemer and Pascal Peeters. (1997). Merging Service Quality and Service Satisfaction: An Empirical Test of an Integrative Model, *Journal of Economic Psychology*, 18, 387-406.

Dick, A.S. and Basu, K. (1994). Customer loyalty: toward an integrated conceptual framework, *Journal of Academy of Marketing Science*, 22, 99-109.

Fornell, Claes. (1992). A National Customer Satisfaction Barometer: The Swedish Experience, *Journal of Marketing*, 56 (January), 6-21.

Gilly, Mary C. and John L. Graham. (1996). International Marketing of Services. In M. Bitner and V. Zeithaml (Ed.) *Services Marketing* (pp. 414-446) New York: McGraw-Hill.

Gronroos, C. (1983). *Strategic Management and Marketing in the Service Sector*, Boston: Marketing Science Institute.

Gronroos, C. (1995). Relationship Marketing: The Strategy Continuum, *Journal of the Academy of Marketing Science*, 23 (4), 252-254.

Gunst, R.F. and R.L. Mason. (1980) *Regression Analysis and Its Application*, New York: Dekker.

Gwinner, K., Grensler, D.M. and Bitner (1998) Relational Benefits in Service Industries, *Journal of the Academy of Marketing Sciences*, 26 (Spring), 101-114.

Hofstede, G. (1980). *Cultural Consequences; International Differences in Work-Related Values*, Beverly Hills: Sage Publication.

Jackson, Barbara B. (1985) *Winning and Keeping Industrial Customers: The Dynamics of Customer Relationships*, Lexington, MA: D.C. Heath and Company.

Jones, Michael A., Mothersbaugh, David L. and Beatty, Sharon E. (2000), Switching Barriers and Repurchase Intentions in Services, *Journal of Retailing*, 70 (2), 259-274.

Jones, Thomas O. and W. Earl Sasser, Jr. (1995). Why Satisfied Customers Defect, *Harvard Business Review*, (November-December), 88-99.

Kasper, H. P. van Helsdunggen, W. de Vries Jr. and P. Helsdingen. (1999), Services Marketing Management: An International Perspective, London: J. Wiley and Sons.

Kohli, A. (1989). Determinants of Influence in Organizational Buying: A Contingency Approach, Journal of Marketing, 53 (July), 50-65.

Malhotra, Nareshk, Francis M. Ugaldo, James Agarwal and Imad Baalbaki. (1994). International Services Marketing: A Comparative Evaluation of the Dimensions of Service Quality between Developed and Developing Countries, *International Marketing Review*, 11 (2), 5-15.

Maute, Manfred F. and William R. Forrester, Jr. (1993). The Structure and Determinants of Consumer Complaint Intentions and Behavior, *Journal of Economics Psychology*, 14, 219-247.

Morgan, Robert M. and Shelby D. Hunt. (1994). The Commitment-Trust Theory of Relationship Marketing, *Journal of Marketing*, 58 (July), 20-38.

Oliver, Richard L. (1980). A Cognitive Model of the Antecedents and Consequences of Satisfaction Decisions, *Journal of Marketing Research*, 17 (November), 460-469.

Oliver, Richard L. and J.E. Swan. (1989). Consumer Perceptions of Interpersonal Equity and Satisfaction in Transactions: A Field Survey Approach, *Journal of Marketing*, 53 (April), 21-35.

Oliver, Richard, L. (1994). Conceptual Issues in the Structural Analysis of Consumption Emotion, Satisfaction, and Quality: Evidence in a Service Setting. In Allen and John (Ed.) *Advances in Consumer Research* (pp. 16-22), Association for Consumer Research.

Oliver, Richard L. (1999). Whence Consumer Loyalty? *Journal of Marketing*, 63, 33-44.

Parasuraman, A., V. Zeithaml and L. Berry. (1988). SERVQUAL: A Multiple Item Scale for Measuring Customer Perceptions of Service Quality, *Journal of Retailing*, 64 (Spring), 12-40.

Patterson, Paul G. and Lester Johnson (1993). Disconfirmation of Expectations and the Gap Model of Service Quality: An Integrated Paradigm, *Journal of Consumer Satisfaction, Dissatisfaction and Complaining Behaviour*, 6, 90-99.

Patterson, Paul G. and Lester Johnson. (1995). Focal Brand Experience and Product Based Norms as Moderators in the Satisfaction Formation Process, *Journal of Consumer Satisfaction, Dissatisfaction and Complaining Behaviour*, 8, 22-31.

Patterson, Paul G., Lester Johnson and Richard Spreng. (1997). Modeling the Determinants of Customer Satisfaction for Business-to-Business Professional Services, *Journal of the Academy of Marketing Science*, 25 (1), 4-17.

Patterson, Paul G. and Tasman Smith (2001). Modeling Relationship Strength Across Service Types in a South-East Asian Context, *International Journal of Service Industry Management*, 12 (7), Forthcoming.

Ping, Robert A. Jr. (1993). The Effects of Satisfaction and Structural Constraints on Retailer Exiting, Voice, Loyalty, Opportunism, and Neglect, *Journal of Retailing*, 69 (3) (Fall), 321-349.

Porter, Michael. (1980). *Competitive Strategy*, New York: The Free Press.

Rusbult, C.E. (1980). Commitment and satisfaction in romantic associations: a test of the investment model, *Journal of Experimental and Social Psychology*, 16, 172-186.

Schutte, Hellmut and Dianna Ciarlante. (1998) *Consumer Behavior in Asia*, London: Macmillan Press.

Sharma, Neeru and Paul G. Patterson. (2000). Switching Costs, Alternative Attractiveness As Moderators of Relationship Commitment in Professional Consumers Services, *International Journal of Service Management*, 11 (5), 470-490.

Triandis, Harry C. (1995) *Individualism and Collectivism*, Boulder: Westview Press.

Tse, D.K. and P.C. Wilton. (1988). Models of Consumer Satisfaction Formation: An Extension, *Journal of Marketing Research*, 25 (May), 204-212.

Usunier, Jean-Claude. (1996). *Marketing Across Culture*, London: Prentice Hall.

Weiss, Allen and Erin Anderson. (1992). Converting from Independent to Employee Salesforces: The Rol., *Journal of Marketing Research*, 29 (1), 101-116.

Winsted, Kathryn Frazer. (1999). Evaluating Service Encounters: A Cross-Cultural and Cross-Industry Exploration, *Journal of Marketing Theory and Practice*, 7 (2), 106-123.

Yi, Y. (1993). The Determinants of Consumer Satisfaction, the Moderating Role of Ambiguity, *Advances in Consumer Research*, 20, 502-506.

Zeithaml, Valarie. (1981). How Consumers Evaluation Processes Differ between Goods and Services. In J.H. Donnelly and W. George (Ed.) *Marketing of Services* (pp. 186-190) Chicago: American Marketing Association.

Zeithaml, Valarie and Mary Jo Bitner. (1996) *Services Marketing*, New York: McGraw-Hill.

Zeithaml, Valarie A.; Berry, Leonard L. and Parasuraman, A. (1996). The behavioral consequences of service quality, *Journal of Marketing*, 60 (April), 31-46.

APPENDIX 1. Demographics Profile of Respondents

Age	%	Sex	%
18-24 Years	11.6	Male	44.2
25-34	32.3	Female	55.8
35-44	24.5		100%
45-54	9.7		
55-64	12.9		
Over 64	9.0		
	100.0%		

OCCUPATION	%
Office Worker	27.0
Professional	27.0
Tradesman	11.2
Home Duties	9.9
Student	11.8
Government Official	4.6
State Enterprise	3.9
Retired	4.6
	100.0%

n = 155

APPENDIX 2. Construct Operationalization and Reliability

Construct and Sample Measures	Range of Cronbach's Alpha across service types
Customer Satisfaction (4 items) Sample items: • I feel good about my decision to use this doctor/hairdresser, etc. • My decision to use this... was a wise one. • I am happy with my decision to use this .... • 7 point rating scale: very dissatisfied to very satisfied	.92-.94
Technical Performance (5 items) • Sample items: • As far as I'm concerned my .... performance is excellent. • My .... usually solves the problem the first time. • The recommendation this .... makes are usually accurate. • Is very knowledgeable about a wide range of conditions. • Their service is always performed without errors.	.85-.92
Functional Performance (5 items) Sample items: • Takes a personal interest in me. • Treats me as an individual, not just another customer. • Is never too busy to be contacted whenever I need something. • Takes the time to understand my specific needs before (providing service). • Is always willing to help me whenever I have a problem.	.91-.95
Switching Costs (4 items) Sample items: • I will lose a friendly and comfortable relationship if I change .... • I will waste a lot of time if I change .... (service provider). • I will have to spend a lot of time explaining my situation to a new .... if I change. • If I change (service provider) there is a risk that the new (hairdresser, mechanic, etc.) won't be as good.	.77-.80

With the exception of the 5-point rating scale for the global satisfaction item, all items were captured on a 5-point Likert scale from Strongly Disagree (1) to Strongly Agree (5).

Perceptions of Factors Driving Success for Multinational Professional Services Firms in Korea

Mary Anne Raymond
John D. Mittelstaedt

SUMMARY. The purpose of this paper is to explore perceptions of the factors that both drive and inhibit success of multinational professional services firms in an Asian market, specifically in Korea. This study examines how multinational professional services firms in Korea are positioned with regard to service attributes. Through surveys and in-depth interviews, researchers explored MNC perceptions of critical dimensions of service success and failure in Korea. Results offer insights into the decision processes of non-Asian firms engaged in services marketing in Asia. *[Article copies available for a fee from The Haworth Document Delivery Service: 1-800-342-9678. E-mail address: <getinfo@haworthpressinc.com> Website: <http://www.HaworthPress.com> © 2001 by The Haworth Press, Inc. All rights reserved.]*

KEYWORDS. Multinational professional services, Korea, service success, trade

Mary Anne Raymond and John D. Mittelstaedt are Assistant Professors, both at Clemson University.

Address correspondence to: Mary Anne Raymond, Assistant Professor, Department of Marketing, College of Business and Public Affairs, Clemson University, Clemson, SC 29634-1325.

The authors thank Dr. Stephen Grove and Dr. Michael Dorsch for their helpful comments.

[Haworth co-indexing entry note]: "Perceptions of Factors Driving Success for Multinational Professional Services Firms in Korea." Raymond, Mary Anne, and John D. Mittelstaedt. Co-published simultaneously in *Journal of International Consumer Marketing* (International Business Press, an imprint of The Haworth Press, Inc.) Vol. 14, No. 1, 2001, pp. 23-41; and: *Asian Dimensions of Services Marketing* (ed: Esther P. Y. Tang, Ricky Y. K. Chan, and Susan H. C. Tai) International Business Press, an imprint of The Haworth Press, Inc., 2001, pp. 23-41. Single or multiple copies of this article are available for a fee from The Haworth Document Delivery Service [1-800-342-9678, 9:00 a.m. - 5:00 p.m. (EST). E-mail address: getinfo@ haworthpressinc.com].

INTRODUCTION

Services account for more than 64 percent of the world's total output (World Bank 2000a) providing increasingly more opportunities for multinational corporations (MNCs) to participate in international trade in the services sector, particularly in rapidly developing markets such as those in East Asia. With over three-fifths of the world's population, East Asia has experienced and continues to show tremendous growth potential in the services industry, where services account for 41 percent of the region's gross domestic product (GDP). With its economic development, economic reforms, and easier access, many multinational firms are investing in, entering, and competing aggressively in South Korea (Korea), where services account for 52 percent of its GDP (World Bank 2000b). However, Korea is described as one of the most difficult markets in the world for international trade, making operating decisions for MNC services providers, particularly professional services providers (e.g., financial institutions, transportation, travel, consulting, advertising, and engineering) difficult ("Background Notes" 2001; World Bank 2000a).

Much of the theory of services marketing, as well as international services marketing, is developed in a Western context. While many studies have examined various aspects of professional services in the U.S. and Europe, there is very little data on the services industry in East Asia, one of the fastest growing regions of the world. Korea, one of the big emerging markets in Asia ("Big Emerging Markets" 2001), poses unique challenges to multinational services firms wishing to standardize professional services across national boundaries. Organizational factors and operating standards that have traditionally been important to MNC services providers may not be as important in the Korean culture where many professional services are relatively new or otherwise unfamiliar. In addition, in a culture where the expectation is that service is assumed to be provided, MNC services providers may have difficulty standardizing their services strategies. Therefore, it is critical to understand how multinational services firms balance the globally competitive requirements of standardization with the local adaptation requirements of their customers in international markets, particularly in emerging markets where the entrance of multinational services providers is relatively new. As such, it is first necessary to determine the perceptions of services firms in emerging markets with regard to their organizational position and various factors that affect success, which may be standardized or adapted based on local market conditions.

The purpose of the study is to explore perceived factors that both drive and inhibit success of multinational professional services firms (services firms focused primarily on business customers) in Korea. Additionally, given the importance, the relative newness, and the tremendous growth of the services industry in Korea, this study examines how professional services firms in Korea position themselves with regard to various service attributes. Specifically, this paper reports on exploratory research intended to better understand the perceptions of professional services MNCs regarding their success and failure in Korea. Accordingly, the remainder of this paper is organized as follows. First, in order to help understand the acceptance of multinational services firms in Korea, the challenges of multinational trade in services and the growth of the services sector in the Korean economy are discussed. This is followed by an overview of the literature on services marketing in East Asia and Korea. Next, we describe the current study and present the findings of the research. Finally, we examine the managerial implications and the future research directions.

BACKGROUND AND LITERATURE REVIEW

Of *Fortune's* 1999 Global 500 firms, more than half (263) were primarily services firms (World Bank 2000a). Future globalization of the world economy will rely on continued growth of services (Keohane and Nye 2000). Dunning (1998) argues that services are a critical component of growth for multinational corporations (MNCs), who increasingly rely on knowledge intensive components of production. "A further indicator of the rising significance of non-material assets as creators or facilitators of wealth is the growth of services, and particularly those which are, themselves, knowledge or information intensive" (p. 47). MNCs are particularly well-suited to provide these kinds of services worldwide, since they are better able to make investments in knowledge intensive enterprises than are local-market competitors. Profiting from the knowledge intensive investments necessary to be competitive in some services industries (e.g., banking, consultancy, up-market hotels, advertising) requires firms to compete globally (Dunning 1993). As in multinational corporations (MNCs) specializing in manufacturing, multinational services firms are also interested in standardizing their offerings to capitalize on production economies of scale while simultaneously meeting the service preferences of local consumers (Fisk, Grove and John 2000).

Relatively speaking, much is known about MNCs who offer services to their international customers to further their trade position in manufactured goods (Dunning 1993). Further, there is considerable interest in those services industries for which there is the greatest trade across national boundaries; that is, those services industries where MNCs have the greatest competitive advantage. Typically, many of the multinational services firms compete in professional business services (e.g., financial, consulting, advertising, accounting, engineering, airlines, up-market hotels, etc.) as the *primary* function of their operations with other businesses being the primary target of their offerings.

The growth of professional business services in international trade has increased the importance of coordinated services strategies for multinational corporations engaged in the trade of services.

The Challenges of Multinational Trade in Services

The bulk of research in the international trade of MNCs has been in the area of manufactured goods. Dunning (1993) points out that lost in this research is the impact of international trade in services. International trade in services is worthy of study since, according the United Nations Centre for Transnational Corporations (1990), the value of the output of foreign owned services has been as great, and in some cases greater, than the output of foreign owned goods.

Because standardization is a key to global competitiveness (Levitt 1983), and because of the intangible, simultaneous and heterogeneous nature of services (Lovelock 1996), it is often easier to standardize the production of goods than services. This creates a challenge for service firms that require large markets to justify their competitive investments. Because of these requirements, some services resemble goods in how they are marketed internationally. Dunning (1993) points out, "In today's technological and economic environment, the leading goods producing firms in such sectors as oil, cars, pharmaceuticals, tires, computers, and consumer electronics can only sustain or advance global competitiveness by selling and producing in the major markets of the world . . . . Most services firms do not need global markets to be competitive. The exceptions are precisely in those sectors in which the proportion of global output accounted for by foreign production is the highest, noticeably in finance and investment banking, some kinds of consultancy, up-market hotels and advertising" (pp. 244-245). In these markets, the challenge is to capitalize on the advantages of standardization, while still meeting the customized needs of services customers.

Some aspects of services are easier to standardize than others. For many services firms, international services marketing poses special challenges, since underlying assumptions of cultural, economic and social similarities among consumers do not hold when national boundaries are crossed. According to Fisk, Grove and John (2000), "When determining strategies for a foreign market, a service organization needs to consider standardization and adaptation possibilities for every aspect of the service offering, including the design of the frontstage and backstage elements" (p. 207). This distinction between frontstage (aspects of service encounters visible to the customer) and backstage (planning and implementation aspects of services invisible to the customer) elements of services may be important to standardization decisions of services MNCs. If a firm decides to "move backstage dimensions of service production

to the frontstage, it requires greater attention to other performance components, such as the actor's roles and their scripts, the audience's participation
and the setting's physical cues" (Grove, Fisk, and Bitner 1992, p. 111). As
such, the management of contact personnel (actors) and their interactions with
customers (audience) as well as the physical surrounding (setting) may vary
across cultures thus requiring MNCs to use an adaptation strategy (Grove,
Fisk, Bitner 1992; Fisk, Grove, John 2000). Given the amount of operational
support and the people involved in planning that are necessary to make a successful service encounter, it may well be that backstage activities are easier to
standardize than their frontstage counterparts.

Growth of the Services Sector in the Korean Economy

Due to economic opportunities, the U.S. Department of Commerce has
identified South Korea (Korea), Indonesia, Taiwan, and the People's Republic
of China (China) as "big emerging markets" ("Big Emerging Markets" 2001).
Korea is a particularly attractive market for professional services firms given
the economic reforms, easier market access, and the growth in its domestic services sector and in foreign investment, as well as its relationships with the U.S.
The services sector of Korea's economy, and foreign investment in Korean
services, have both grown in the 1990s. However, as shown in Table 1, during
the seven year period, 1993-1999, growth in services in Korea averaged 6.4
percent while the corresponding overall growth in gross domestic product
(GDP) averaged only 5.5 percent (*Advance Report* 2000). Services are an increasingly important sector of the Korean economy and most of the growth in
services is from MNCs that are entering East Asian markets. Additionally, the
number of U.S. firms that made new investments in the Korean service economy increased in number and dollar value in the years, 1995-97 ("Economic
Statistics" 1999), indicating that services represent a growing sector for MNC
investment in Korea (see Table 2).

State of the Literature on Services Marketing in Asia and Korea

While there exists a growing body of literature on the internationalization of
services marketing (Vandermerwe and Chadwick 1989; Erramilli 1989; 1991;
Darhinger 1991; Clark, Rajaratnam and Smith 1996; Kotabe, Murray and
Javalgi 1998; Coviello and Martin 1999), only limited research exists on services marketing in Asia, in general, and Korea, in particular. A few exceptions
include Min and Min's (1996) work on Korean hotels, Raymond and Rylance's
(1996) research on professional services in Korea, and Ha's (1998) comparison of advertising appeals for services firms in the U.S. and Hong Kong.

Min and Min (1996) studied the hotel industry in Korea and found that the
courtesy of the staff was one of the most important attributes. They proposed

TABLE 1. GDP Growth in Korea, by Industrial Sectors

	GDP Growth	Services	Manfact.	Agricul.
1993	5.5	7.2	5.4	−4.5
1994	8.3	10.3	10.8	0.2
1995	8.9	9.6	11.3	6.6
1996	6.8	7.8	6.8	3.3
1997	5.0	5.4	6.6	4.6
1998	−6.7	−7.2	−7.2	−6.6
1999	10.7	11.7	21.8	4.7
7 Year Average	5.5	6.4	7.9	1.2

Source: Advance Report of Major Statistics, Korean National Statistical Office, April 2000

TABLE 2. New U.S. Investments in Korean Services, 1995-1997 (in Million Dollars)

	1995		1996		1997	
	Number	Amount	Number	Amount	Number	Amount
Services	124	321	127	351	127	2,612
	(77.0)	(49.8)	(76.0)	(40.1)	(70.1)	(81.9)
Banking	3	66	2	52	1	12.4
Trade	44	23	40	48	38	53.7
Insurance	-	-	1	3	1	5.7
Hotels	5	90	3	99	12	2,453
Restaurants	5	6	6	3	3	0.345
Other	43	110	44	44	50	63.5
Manufacturing	37	324	40	525	52	577
	(23.0)	(50.2)	(24.0)	(59.9)	(28.7)	(18.0)
Agriculture & Fisheries	-	-	-	-	2	0.257
Total	161	645	167	876	181	3,189

Source: "Economic Statistics," Embassy of Korea, Washington, DC, January, 1999.
"( )" represent % of total foreign investment by industrial sector

that service performance measures should be used to compare performance of service providers against service leaders. In their study on the evaluation and selection of professional services firms in Korea, Raymond and Rylance (1996) found that client satisfaction was always an important factor in a firm's organization, although very few companies said they listened to their customers. They also found that services were not understood in Korea and that many firms were hesitant to "outsource" or pay for services. Ha's (1998) study examined advertising appeals by services firms in Hong Kong and the U.S. In Hong Kong, many advertisements emphasized stylishness or popularity of services, while advertisements in the U.S. emphasized consumer's intelligence in service provider selection. Each of these studies lends insight into the nature of the competitive environment for services marketing in Korea.

The limited amount of research on services marketing in Korea may be due, in part, to the fact that Korean services traditionally have been tied to the *chaebols,* large conglomerates with in-house services (Raymond and Rylance 1996), limiting access for non-Korean firms to compete in the Korean services market. Built on important friendship and kinship ties, these conglomerates enforce service quality through personal relationships. These "kintracts" have simultaneously limited the access of foreigners to important service markets and minimized the demand for external services marketing firms in Korea. However, with the collapse of many chaebol relationships during the 1998 Asian economic crisis, and a subsequent easing of restrictions on foreign investment, demand for foreign investments increased, creating services marketing opportunities and a new interest in services marketing research. Still, the number of foreign providers (MNCs) of professional business services in Korea is limited.

Unique Challenges of Services in Korea and Asia

Korea presents unique challenges to MNCs interested in the marketing of services. First, the tightly knit economy limits the opportunity for foreign firms to establish themselves in service industries. Raymond and Rylance (1996) found that many firms must establish themselves in partnership with Korean firms in order to gain access to the market. However, the foreign partner does not always have a say in running the business, especially when they partner with bigger and more successful Korean firms (De Mente 1994).

Second, the collectivist nature of Korean culture (Hofstede 1980) affects expectations of service providers, and service satisfaction. Expectations and standards may be higher, or lower, than those found in individualist countries like the U.S. when customers judge service value in the context of collective expectations. While both of these aspects provide challenges for MNC service providers operating in Korea, they are not dissimilar from conditions in other Asian countries, such as Keiretsus in Japan (Cateora and Graham 1999) or the collectivism of Chinese culture (Bond and Hwang 1986).

Because collectivism manifests itself in Korean culture, management styles tend to work against the inclusion of foreigners in the business process. Western principles of management are taught and emulated in Korean universities, but because many of these principles are in conflict with traditional Korean values and with the chaebols, there is often a great discrepancy between what Koreans see as guiding management principles and external perceptions of these principles at work. Consequently, while it may be possible to derive a fairly accurate picture of the rational economic drivers of organizations, social drivers may be more difficult to ascertain from traditional marketing services quality indicators. Koreans tend to place higher value on relationships than do Americans (Foster 1992; Setton 1995). Because individuals tend to define themselves within a web of social relations, there exists no clear distinction between "public" and "private," "business" and "pleasure." This emphasis on human relationships manifests itself in different approaches to management issues like staff relations, leadership, decision-making, employee selection and contractual agreements. The amount of trust Koreans feel for each other is directly related to proximity of relationships (Moran and Stripp 1991). Consequently, the greatest trust is reserved for close family members, followed by friends and colleagues. The lowest levels of trust are shown to those removed culturally or geographically. Lowest on this scale are foreigners. Reflecting these tendencies, a Gallup survey of 18 nations found Korea to have the lowest tolerance for value systems other than their own (Setton 1995).

These external challenges in Korea may pose different operating decisions than those in other markets where the MNC does business. As a result, factors within the organization and operating standards that have traditionally been important to MNC service providers may not be as important in the Korean culture where many professional services are new or otherwise unfamiliar. In addition, in a culture where service may be considered expected to be provided, companies may have difficulty standardizing their services strategies. If service delivery does not meet with customer expectations, or fails to reflect the service firm's communications or marketing promise, disappointment or failure will seriously damage reputations and hinder future business opportunities. Our interest is in the perceptions of how MNC service providers feel they must operate to compete locally, while still capitalizing on the advantages of standardization. As such, we are interested in how service firms are positioned with regard to service attributes and what are the perceived drivers and inhibitors for success of multinational service firms in Korea.

CURRENT STUDY

Raymond and Rylance (1996) examined the importance of service aspects in the evaluation and selection of professional services providers in Korea.

They also looked at the importance of various factors, such as the physical environment (frontstage activity) and employee's attitudes (actors) in an organization. Based on their results, this study reexamines various aspects of professional services providers in Korea.

Purpose of the Study

The purpose of this exploratory study is to determine the organizational position of MNC services firms against a variety of service attributes. Given the unique challenges in the Korean market and the orientation of each firm, the study seeks to determine what factors drive the success of MNC service providers in Korea and, conversely, what factors inhibit their success. Specifically, the study seeks to answer the following research questions concerning professional service providers in Korea.

Research Question 1: How are multinational services firms positioned with regard to various service attributes?

Research Question 2: What factors do MNCs perceive to be most important in determining the success of professional services in Korea?

Research Question 3: What factors limit the success of professional services in Korea?

Methodology

Two steps were followed to answer the research questions identified. First, top executives at multinational services firms operating in Korea were surveyed to determine their perceptions of the professional services environment in Korea. Second, based on the initial results and the desire for additional feedback, in-depth interviews were conducted with top executives at five U.S. and British services firms. Through the surveys and in-depth interviews this study offers insights into the decision processes of non-Asian firms engaged in services marketing in Korea. As such, this study provides information that multinational services firms may use to contrast and compare against Western benchmarks and other markets where they do business.

Survey Sample

In order to examine the organizational position of multinational services firms and the factors perceived to enhance their success or inhibit them from being successful in the service industry in Korea, a sample was selected from multinational service providers with offices in Seoul, Korea. The sampling frame consisted of service firms listed as members of either the American Chamber of Commerce in Korea or the British Chamber of Commerce in Korea that had a local top executive identified in the directory. One hundred and three service firms, including financial institutions, management consultant firms, advertising agencies, research firms, airlines, up-market hotels, and engineering service firms that had a local top executive contact were identified in the Chamber of Commerce directories. Three firms were consulted in the development of the survey and were not part of the sample. As a result, 100 foreign services providers doing business in Korea were selected to receive surveys.

Survey Instrument

Given the recent growth in the services industry in Korea, the importance of relationships, and the unique challenges in the Korean culture, respondents were asked to indicate their organization's position on a scale of 1 to 5 (with descriptors given) on a variety of service attributes. The descriptors typically reflected a range of understanding that firms may have on factors related to Korean culture that affect the development of service offerings and doing business in Korea. The attributes reflected activities/concerns that were considered important in doing business in other markets. Some of the attributes involved internal (backstage) issues such as employee loyalty, employee attitude, and service culture. Others were externally determined service attributes and may have appeared more visible to the clients (frontstage decisions), such as customer orientation, customer value and listening to the customer. For example, when asked to position their organization on "listening to the customer," the descriptors ranged from "1" being an ad hoc identification of Korean customer expectations and requirements to "5" where a firm had a range of both formal and informal mechanisms for identifying customer expectations, which were then utilized for Korean service design and service standards.

Respondents were also asked to select and rank the top three factors that they thought were important drivers for success in the Korean service economy. Twelve options were offered, each reflecting factors of service success determined in preliminary interviews and previous studies (Raymond and Rylance 1996). Many of the factors also reflected typical corporate objectives, such as "to be a leader in quality," and "to reduce operating costs." Respondents also had the opportunity to indicate and specify other factors of service success. Finally, respondents were asked to indicate and rank the top three factors they considered as inhibitors of service success in Korea. Seven factors were listed reflecting some of the challenges facing multinational service providers operating in foreign markets, such as "international competition" and "government policies." Again, respondents had the opportunity to specify other factors that inhibited their success in the service industry in Korea. Combined, these findings are expected to provide a clearer picture of international service success and failure in Korea.

Interview Sample

Based on the results of the survey, five multinational services firms in different industries were chosen for structured in-depth follow-up interviews. These firms were selected based on their willingness to participate in a follow-up survey and the representation of different industries. The industries represented in the follow-up interviews included a consulting firm, an airline, a bank, an advertising firm, and an up-market hotel. All of the firms focused primarily on serving business customers and were large multinational corporations, each a worldwide leader in its industry, and two were *Fortune* Global 500 firms.

RESULTS

Results of the Survey

The top executive identified at each service firm listed in the Chamber of Commerce directories was contacted by telephone prior to being sent a survey. Based on these telephone calls, it was determined that most of the executives in the sampling frame preferred to receive the survey by fax. A copy of the survey was faxed to the top executive identified at all 100 service firms in the sample. Five surveys were returned because the firms said that most of their services were pre-arranged through contracts in the United States. Therefore, the effective sample size was 95. A total of 31 usable surveys were returned for a response rate of 33.0 percent.

Table 3 reports on the MNCs organizational position in Korea with regard to a number of service attributes. The service attribute where the multinational services firms felt that they were best positioned for the service industry in Korea was the firm's organization for service design (a back stage decision). This was followed by employee loyalty and having a customer orientation. Results in Table 3 indicate that firms are positioned better on many internal factors (back stage decisions) of service quality are than they are on external factors (front stage decisions), such as listening to the customer and meeting customer needs. This suggests that firms focus first on organizational needs, which may be easier to standardize and many of which may be determined in their home country (market) and focus second on customer needs, which may be different in foreign markets and may require adaptation strategies.

TABLE 3. Organizational Position on Service Attributes

Internal Service Attribute	Mean Score
Organization for Service Design	4.45
Employee Loyalty	3.97
Employee Attitude	3.90
Vision of Quality Service	3.81
Innovation/Development of New Services	3.70
Service Culture	3.65
Designing Service	3.55
Mean	3.86
External Service Attributes	**Mean Score**
Customer Orientation	3.97
Customer Value	3.94
Market Awareness	3.81
Service Meets Customer Needs	3.45
Listening to Customer	3.37
Mean	3.70

Table 4 reports on those drivers that MNCs perceive to be important for service success in Korea. Respondents indicated and ranked the top three factors for establishing themselves in the Korean market. Of the 12 factors, being a leader in quality was ranked the highest with almost three quarters of all respondents identifying this as an important ingredient for service success in Korea. Six of every ten executives responding to the survey indicated that being a leader in customer service was a driver of service success, while four in ten focused on being a leader in value for the money. These latter results are interesting, given that external factors (frontstage decisions) of service, such as listening to the customer, were rated so low by firms when determining their organizational (market) position.

Table 5 reports on the greatest inhibitors to service success in Korea. Firms were asked to indicate and rank those factors most likely to inhibit the success of a foreign services firm in Korea. Three quarters of the respondents indicated that the greatest barrier to success was the inability to find trained service employees. This finding was expected given the relative newness and growth of the service industry in Korea as well as the expectation of service being provided. Six in ten executives reported that government policies inhibited their ability to succeed in the service sector. It is important to note that government policy limits the number of work visas that MNCs can obtain for foreign employees, necessitating the hiring of Korean nationals who may be inexperi-

TABLE 4. Drivers of Service/Business in Korea

Factor	% Ranking
To be a leader in quality	74%
To be a leader in customer service	58
To be a leader in value for money	39
To reduce operating costs	29
To launch new services fastest	13
To be a leader in innovation	10
To invest in information technology	6
To maximize market share	6
To survive the next 12 months	6
To be highly profitable	6
To satisfy employees	3
To respond to government objectives	0

Note: percentages exceed 100% because respondents gave up to 3 rankings

enced in the service industry. Interestingly, of the six inhibiting factors selected by at least 10% of the sample, only one (ability to implement change quickly) was within the control of firms. Service firms lacked the ability to control or influence any of the other important inhibitors to service success.

Results of the In-Depth Interviews

To further explore issues of services marketing in Korea, five in-depth interviews were conducted with leading foreign services firms in Korea. Interviews focused on three issues: internal training and organization of services marketing; dealing with Korean clients as an outsider to Korean culture; and the ability of firms to adapt to changing service expectations in Korea.

Internal Training: None of the five companies interviewed had a formalized program for developing the company's service philosophy or policy as it relates to the Korean market. Each company had a mission statement, vision and values statement, service manuals and other standard corporate material, which they used in offices around the world. However, no guidelines were developed specifically for Korea.

No firm interviewed (or surveyed, for that matter) had an extensive training program aimed at training foreign executives on the unique dimensions of the Korean market from a service quality perspective. Given the availability of skilled workers in the service industry, it was interesting that all of the firms interviewed had their Korean staff learn by example from either senior expatriates or senior Korean employees whom the company believed understood and demonstrated the Western ideals of service.

TABLE 5. Inhibitors to Achieving Service/Business Success in Korea

Factor	% Ranking
Availability of trained/skilled people	74%
Government policy	61
Ability to implement change quickly	39
International competition	23
Capital market restrictions	16
Cost of living in Korea	10
Internal company bureaucracy	3
Korean partner interference	3
No economy of scale in Korea	3
Low/Unacceptable margins	3
Communications problems	3
Industry image	3
Wrong priorities from headquarters	3
Foreign exchange fluctuation	3
Vulnerability to takeover/acquisition	0

Note: percentages exceed 100% because respondents gave up to 3 rankings

Dealing with Korean Clients: Dealing with clients required that MNC services firms understand and adapt to the managerial style of those Korean firms (clients). Interviews indicated this was a particularly difficult dimension of services marketing for foreign firms. It was felt that one reason for this difficulty may be that many Korean chaebols still operate a career management system called "hobong" in which the employee hierarchy is determined by age, length of service, education and relationships, or "chong." Under this system the ability or knowledge of a worker is only one of a number of criteria for filling management positions. According to the respondents, many Korean companies are staffed with employees in positions about which they know little. One component of Korean culture and the chaebol system is the belief that age equals wisdom and ability. This creates additional problems for a foreign firm with young employees, especially at the management level. In these cases firms found that traditional customer feedback systems offered little guidance for improved service quality. Only one of the firms interviewed had a formal customer feedback system. The other firms relied on informal feedback when meeting directly with the customer. Unfortunately, Koreans' focus on harmony (Moran and Stripp 1991) as well as the collectivism aspect of Korean culture may limit the usefulness of such information.

Adapting Services to the Korean Environment: The third factor relevant to foreign firms doing business in Korea is the apparent difficulty of implementing and adapting programs to the unique challenges of the Korean culture. A reoccurring comment through all interviews was the severe resistance to change in Korea. According to one executive, resistance to change was the number one hurdle for his firm in Korea. Change was met with emotional and often irrational opposition, especially when it was seen as coming from a foreign firm. Due to Korea's resistance to change and its limited experience with services industries, many foreign companies have had to adapt by spending an exhaustive amount of time educating and communicating with Korean clients on the benefits of outside service providers and how they can help the Korean company.

DISCUSSION AND CONCLUSIONS

The results of this study indicate that professional services MNCs operating in Korea focus first on internal (back stage), rather than external (front stage), activities and stakeholders. While they profess an interest in quality and customer service, issues important to positioning suggest a greater concern for issues of their firm's internal organization and training. The absence of a service tradition in Korean culture requires that foreign services providers create a service culture within the context of Korean collectivism. Korean manifestations of collectivist culture suggest that success depends on building human relationships, becoming part of the extended family, and shedding the label of "foreigner." All of these require an internal (front stage) focus for professional services firms. Belonging is a necessary first step for success. However, problems that executives in Korea have had in convincing their headquarters to adjust their operations to the Korean market have been well-documented (DeMente 1994).

Second, the focus on internal (back stage) organization indicates differences between Korean and Western services marketing orientations. Western firms organize their structure to reflect customer demand (Fisk, Grove and John 2000). For these firms, external (front stage) focus is the necessary prerequisite for services success. The results of this study suggest that, at least in Korea, internal (back stage) focus is the necessary condition for services success. This may be due in part to the idea that indeed back stage decisions (planning and implementation aspects of services that are invisible to the customer) are easier to standardize than front stage activities (aspects of the service encounters visible to the customer) (Fisk, Grove, and John 2000). In addition, as Grove, Fisk, and Bitner (1992) noted, the structure may not change, but it is important for services marketers to adapt the performance to different cultures. The findings of this study emphasize the unique challenges facing professional service providers in Korea. As such, while managers may standardize some aspects of services in international markets, the aspects to be standardized may be different from market to market, based on the operating environment.

Third, with the exception of the ability to respond quickly, factors leading to services failure all lie beyond the control of firms. (For all practical purposes, the ability to respond quickly also lies beyond the control of local managers of MNCs operating in multiple national markets.) These conditions may change with the growth of professional services in Korea, but currently they provide a context for managerial decisions. This creates a paradox for services providers: while internal issues are necessary conditions for services success, sufficient conditions all lay beyond the control of most firms.

IMPLICATIONS AND FUTURE RESEARCH

Given the growth of the services industry in Korea and the unique challenges facing multinational services providers, the results of this study have implications for the standardization and adaptation of services strategies in East Asian markets such as Korea. As previously mentioned, back stage activities may be easier to standardize, but it is critical for services providers to adapt their strategies to each cultural setting.

Continued growth in services in Korea will require foreign participation in Korea's service economy and it is expected that additional MNC service providers will enter the Korean market. As such, the results of this study provide many insights and implications for managers of MNCs, particularly professional services firms, operating in or planning to operate in Korea. Most critical among these implications are those related to adapting strategies in order to operate successfully given many uncontrollable factors and unique challenges of doing business in Korea. While restrictions for foreign companies are easing in Korea, government regulations continue to affect services providers. The limited availability of work visas will continue to affect professional services providers. Given the lack of a service "attitude" and highly skilled employees, many MNCs turn to foreigners for their workforce. Foreign service providers will have to work within these limitations and develop strategies for recruiting and training Korean nationals as contact personnel (actors).

The Korean culture and the "lack" of a service focus may affect the acceptance and success of service firms. However, as the services economy grows so will the acceptance of service providers. Image and reputation, which are of paramount importance in the Korean culture, are two factors that managers must develop for acceptance. Therefore, it is important for firms to establish relationships in the Korean community. This might entail recruiting from highly regarded colleges and universities in Korea in order to establish a relationship with other alumni, which in turn should lead to more business.

The close relationships and culture in Korea also present other unique challenges for professional services providers in Korea. For example, it is considered against the culture to complain or express dissatisfaction, so firms may not even be aware of problems or try to measure customer satisfaction. Therefore, MNCs may find it beneficial to develop a client feedback system that allows them to measure performance accurately. The close relationships and circle of "friends" may also lead to questions about service providers and other people being so friendly because the Koreans are not accustomed to this type of treatment. However, the respect for superiors and elders, that is such a critical aspect of the Korean culture, is equally important in the services industry. Many of the formalities of the culture can be transferred over to the services firm. The employees have to understand the importance of a "service" attitude and their role in making the firm a success. As such, communication within and outside of the firm is absolutely essential if a professional services provider wants to succeed in Korea. Both internal (back stage) and external (front stage) marketing decisions are key strategic issues. Services providers must create a sense of belonging among employees, a critical aspect of a collectivist culture. Firms must learn to manage expectations by good communication. This will help organizations gain acceptance and build their client base.

The findings of this study make an important contribution to the literature on doing business in a rapidly emerging market, such as Korea. The perceptions of MNC service providers regarding actors that may drive and/or inhibit success are important for managers. While many East Asian cultures are similar, studies should be conducted in other markets to see if the findings are similar. It is particularly important to examine other emerging markets, such as Taiwan, and compare professional services providers in emerging markets with highly industrialized markets such as Japan. Further, as the growth in the services sector continues and more restrictions on foreign trade are lifted, it is critical to reexamine various aspects of the service industry, particularly the back stage and front stage activities to see where standardization is possible.

REFERENCES

Advance Report of Major Statistics (2000), Korean National Statistical Office, April.

"Background Notes: Korea" (2000), U.S. Department of State, Bureau of East Asian and Pacific Affairs, Washington, DC (June).

"Big Emerging Markets" (2000), U.S. Department of Commerce, inclang.com/inclang5.htm, January 2.

Bond, M.H., and K.K. Hwang (1986), "The Social Psychology of Chinese People," in *The Psychology of the Chinese People*, edited by M.H. Bond, Hong Kong: Oxford University Press, 213-266.

Cateora, P.R., and J.L. Graham (1999), *International Marketing, 10th Edition*. Boston: Irwin/McGraw-Hill.

Clark, T., D. Rajaratnam, and T. Smith (1996), "Toward a Theory of International Services: Marketing Intangibles in a World of Nations, *Journal of International Marketing*, 4 (2), 9-28.

Coviello, N. E., and K. A.-M. Martin (1999), "Internationalization of Service SMEs: An Integrated Perspective from the Engineering Consulting Sector," *Journal of International Marketing*, 7 (4), 42-66.

Darhinger, L.D. (1991), "Marketing Services Internationally: Barriers and Management Strategies," *Journal of Services Marketing*, 5 (3), 5-17.

DeMente, B.L. (1994), *Korean Etiquette and Ethics in Business*, 2nd Edition. Chicago: NTC Business Books.

Dunning, J.H. (1993), *The Globalization of Business*. London: Routledge.

Dunning, J.H. (1998), "Location and the Multinational Enterprise: A Neglected Factor?" *Journal of International Business Studies*, 29 (1): 45-66.

"Economic Statistics" (1999), Embassy of Korea, Washington, DC, January.

Erramilli, K.M. (1989), "Entry Mode Choice in Service Industries," *International Marketing Review*, 7 (5), 50-62.

_____ (1991), "The Experience Factor in Foreign Market Entry Behavior of Service Firms," *Journal of International Business Studies*, 22 (3), 479-501.

Evans, P., and T.S. Wurster (2000), *Blown to Bits*. Boston: Harvard Business Press.

Fisk, R.P., S.J. Grove, and J. John (2000), *Interactive Services Marketing*. Boston: Houghton-Mifflin Company.

Ford, John, John F. Tanner, Jr., and Warren French (1989), "Responding to Japanese Competitive Moves," *Proceedings*, AMA Winter Educator's Conference.

Foster, D.A. (1992), *Bargaining Across Borders*. New York: McGraw-Hill, Inc.

Grove, S.J., R.P. Fisk, and M.J. Bitner (1992), "Dramatizing the Service Experience," *Advances in Services Marketing and Management*, JAI Press, Volume 1, 91-121.

Garten, J.E. (1997), *The Big Ten: The Big Emerging Markets and How They Will Change Our Lives*. New York: Basic Books.

Ha, L. (1998), "Advertising Appeals Used by Services Marketers: A Comparison Between Hong Kong and the United States," *The Journal of Services Marketing*, 12 (2), 98-112.

Hofstede, G. (1980), "Motivation, Leadership, and Organization: Do American Theories Apply Abroad?" *Organizational Dynamics*, 42-63.

ICN Language Services (2000), "Big Emerging Markets," <www.icnlang.com> 20 April.

Keohane, R.O., and J.S. Nye, Jr. (2000), "Globalization: What's New? What's Not? (And So What?)," *Foreign Policy*, 118, 104-119.

Korean National Statistics Office (2000), "Advance Report of Major Statistics," <www.nso.go.kr/stat/other/e-speed.htm> 20 April.

Kotabe, M., J.Y. Murray, and R.G. Javalgi (1998), "Global Sourcing of Serices and Market Performance: An Emprical Investigation," *Journal of International Marketing*, 6 (4), 10-31.

Levitt, T. (1983), "The Globalization of Markets," *Harvard Business Review*, May-June: 92-102.

Lovelock, C.H. (1996), *Services Marketing*, Third Edition. Upper Saddle River, New Jersey: Prentice Hall.

Min, H., and H. Min (1996), "Competitive Benchmarking of Korean Luxury Hotels Using Analytic Hierarchy Process and Competitive Gap Analysis," *The Journal of Services Marketing*, 10 (3), 58-72.

Moran, R.T., and W.G. Stripp (1991), *Dynamics of Successful International Business Negotiations*. Houston: Gulf Publishing Company.

Raymond, M.A., and W. Rylance (1996), "Evaluation and Management of Professional Services in Korea." in *Marketing in Asia Pacific and Beyond*, edited by C.R. Taylor, Vol. 7 of *Advances in International Marketing*. Greenwich, Connecticut: JAI Press, 111-125.

Setton, M. (1995) "Characteristics of Korean Management." Working Paper.

Vandermerwe, S., and M. Chadwick (1989), "The Internationalization of Services," *The Services Industry Journal*, 9 (1), 79-93.

World Bank (2000a), *World Development Report, 2000-2001: Attacking Poverty*. New York: Oxford University Press.

World Bank (2000b), *2000 World Development Indicators*. New Work: The World Bank.

Reference Group Influence and Perceived Risk in Services Among Working Women in Singapore: A Replication and Extension

Subhash C. Mehta

Ashok K. Lalwani

Lisa Ping

SUMMARY. Although widely acclaimed as one of the most important determinant of an individual's behavior, reference group influence is hardly explored in the services sector. This study investigated reference group influence on services using a research paradigm originally proposed by Bearden and Etzel (1982), who recognized that social visibility and exclusivity were important factors influencing reference group influence. In addition, perceived risk of services on consumer behavior was also explored. The study was conducted on working women in Singapore, who, due to their affluence and spending power, are the focus of marketers in the region. Results indicated that informational reference group was the most pervasive form of influence for all types of services studied. Further, publicly consumed services were found to have higher

Subhash C. Mehta is Professor of Marketing, Department of Marketing, National University of Singapore. Ashok K. Lalwani is Lecturer, Department of Marketing, University of Florida. Lisa Ping is Underwriter, General & Cologne Reinsurance Group, Singapore.

Address correspondence to: Ashok K. Lalwani, Department of Marketing, P.O Box 117155, Gainesville FL 32611, USA (E-mail: lalwani@ufl.edu).

[Haworth co-indexing entry note]: "Reference Group Influence and Perceived Risk in Services Among Working Women in Singapore: A Replication and Extension." Mehta, Subhash C., Ashok K. Lalwani, and Lisa Ping. Co-published simultaneously in *Journal of International Consumer Marketing* (International Business Press, an imprint of The Haworth Press, Inc.) Vol. 14, No. 1, 2001, pp. 43-65; and: *Asian Dimensions of Services Marketing* (ed: Esther P. Y. Tang, Ricky Y. K. Chan, and Susan H. C. Tai) International Business Press, an imprint of The Haworth Press, Inc., 2001, pp. 43-65. Single or multiple copies of this article are available for a fee from The Haworth Document Delivery Service [1-800-342-9678, 9:00 a.m. - 5:00 p.m. (EST). E-mail address: getinfo@haworthpressinc.com].

reference group influence than privately consumed services. However, in some services, certain unique perspectives were noted due to the nature of the service in question. Luxury services were also found to have higher reference group influence and financial and psychological risk than necessity services. Implications for service marketers are discussed. *[Article copies available for a fee from The Haworth Document Delivery Service: 1-800-342-9678. E-mail address: <getinfo@haworthpressinc.com> Website: <http://www.HaworthPress.com>* © *2001 by The Haworth Press, Inc. All rights reserved.]*

KEYWORDS. Reference group influence, consumer services, Singapore, perceived risk

Others' influence has long been recognized as an important determinant of an individual's behavior (Sherif, 1936; Asch, 1953). Substantial evidence indicates that purchase decisions are made in and influenced by the social environment (Stafford, 1966; Cacanougher and Bruce, 1971). The pervasive use of spokespersons in advertisements confirms the widely held belief that individuals who are admired or who belong to a group, in which other individuals aspire to be, can exercise influence on consumer's information processing, attitude formation and purchase behavior.

Although the realization of reference group influence has led to a proliferation of research in psychology, sociology (Asch, 1953; Sherif, 1936) and consumer behavior (Venkatesan, 1966; Bearden and Etzel, 1982), reference group influence in the services sector has hardly been explored. This study seeks to investigate reference group influence for services using a research framework originally proposed by Bearden and Etzel (1982) who recognized that social visibility and exclusivity were important factors affecting the extent of reference group influence. Researchers have also ignored the effects of perceived risk on reference group influence. This study attempts to fill these gaps.

CONTEXT OF STUDY

In recent years, the services sector has experienced explosive growth worldwide. In fact, the service industry has undergone such tremendous growth that researchers have noted that it will reshape the structure of the economy and the competition. In Singapore, the total number of establishments in this sector have more than tripled in the last two decades and the number of employees more than doubled (Anonymous, 1996). Given the growing economic and social influence of services, it is critical that the dynamics affecting service decisions be understood before effective strategies can be implemented. Unfortunately, reference group influence has received limited attention from service researchers.

This study investigates consumer's susceptibility to reference group influence on four categories of services. The perceived risk for purchases of different social visibility and exclusivity have also been explored. The study also seeks to explore the relationship between social visibility, service exclusivity (service conspicousness) and perceived risk (if any).

The characteristics of intangibility, perishability, heterogeneity, and simultaneous production and consumption lead services to possess only a few search qualities and many experiential and credential qualities. Because services are conceptualized as experiential (Booms and Bitner, 1981; Lovelock 1981), consumer search process for services is more difficult than that of goods, which makes consumer decision making and evaluation more complex. In addition, the characteristics of intangibility, seperability, perishability and simultaneous production and consumption lead to increased perceived risk (Sheth, 1974; Guseman, 1981; Bateson, 1992), which in turn affect the way consumers make purchase decisions (Turley and LeBlanc, 1993).

Many authors have found the concept of perceived risk to be a useful framework for analyzing service purchase behavior. Specifically, services like hairdressing, life insurance, legal services, dry cleaners and banks have been most frequently studied (Mitchell and Greatorex, 1993). These studies examined the type of risks perceived and risk relievers adopted by consumers and found that consumers are more likely to use reference groups for services than for goods (Guseman, 1981). Also, the greater the perceived risk of the purchase decision, higher is the degree of personal influence (Perry and Hamm, 1969). Studies have consistently revealed that word-of-mouth is the most important source of risk reduction and has a greater impact than mass media communications because of the trust involved and the opportunity for clarification and feedback. Studies have also revealed that for products dominant in social aspects, interpersonal influence is a more important component of information acquisition than objective or impersonal sources (Migley, 1983; Price and Feick, 1984). Hence, consumers who wish to reduce prechoice uncertainty may be compelled to seek information from other individuals who have experienced the service directly or indirectly.

Swartz and Stephens (1984) examined the relationship between perceived risk and information search and found that there was no relationship between the two for financial institutions, hairdressers and doctors. A weak relationship was found between perceived performance risk and amount of search for hairdressers, while no relationship existed for financial institutions and doctors. Given the mixed results for perceived risk, it appears timely to investigate how consumers perceive risk in different services.

A measure of overall risk can be obtained as a combination of uncertainty and consequences. The consequences component has been subdivided into six types of loss (i) financial, (ii) performance, (iii) physical, (iv) social, (v) psychological and (vi) time (Garner 1986).

REFERENCE GROUP CONSTRUCT

The term "reference group" was first operationalized by Hyman (1942) who, while investigating social status, asked respondents about the people with whom they compared themselves. This characterization was subsequently refined by future researchers. Deutsch and Gerard (1955) distinguished two types of social influence. The first being "informational social influence" which is to obtain evidence about the true state of some aspect of the individual's environment. The second type is normative social influence, which is the influence to conform to the expectations of another person or group (Burnkrant and Cousineau, 1975). Kelley (1947) distinguished between reference groups as *comparative groups,* which are used to compare for self-appraisal purposes, and *normative groups, which* are used as sources of personal norms, attitudes and values.

Kelman (1961) proposed that social influence operates through one or more of three distinct processes–(1) internalization, (2) identification, and (3) compliance. *Internalization* occurs when the individual accepts influence because the content is perceived as a means to attaining his goals. *Identification* occurs when an individual adopts a behavior or opinion derived from another because the relationship between the individual and the other is beneficial to the individual's self-concept. Advertisers use celebrities to exploit the identification process, as individuals emulate the attitudes or behavior of another person or group, simply because they aspire to be like that person or group (Friedman & Friedman, 1979). *Compliance* occurs when the individual conforms to the expectation of another in order to receive a reward or avoid a punishment mediated by that person.

Park and Lessig (1977), extending the work of Deutsch and Gerard (1955) and Kelman (1961), defined a reference group to be *an actual or imaginary individual or group, which has significant influence upon an individual's evaluations, aspirations or behavior.* They identified three types of reference groups influence namely (1) utilitarian, (2) value expressive, and (3) informational.

Utilitarian reference group influence is based on an individual's attempts to comply with the preferences or expectations of another individual or group if it is believed that (1) they mediate significant rewards or punishments, (2) his behavior will be visible or known to others, and (3) he is motivated to realize the reward or avoid the punishment. *Value-expressive* reference group influence occurs when an individual adopts a behavior or opinion of another in order to enhance or support his self-concept through referent identification. An individual may adopt a behavior or opinion of the referent either to resemble the reference group or simply out of liking for the reference group. Utilitarian and value-expressive influences together form the normative influence.

Informational reference group influence is similar to Deutsch and Gerard's (1955) definition of informational social influence and is based on the desire to make informed decisions. The influence is internalized if it is perceived as enhancing the individual's knowledge of his environment and if the source is perceived to be credible. An individual may seek information from an informational reference group either by searching information from opinion leaders or experts or by observing the behavior of significant others, e.g., by observing the brands of shoes worn by athletes. Sport shoe companies give hundreds of dollars worth of equipment to running clubs, hoping to gain favorable exposure with local joggers (Lisko, 1983). People use other's product evaluations as a source of information about the product (Burnkrant and Cousineau, 1975).

Venkatesan (1966) studied the influence of group pressure and the effects of choice restriction on the consumer decision-making process, and found that individuals tend to conform to the group norm and accept information provided by their peer groups on the quality, style and other product attributes which were difficult to evaluate objectively. Thus, individuals appeared to act in a manner that was consistent with the social group with which they identified.

From marketing and consumer behavior perspectives, the influence of reference groups on individual behavior is often manifested in the types of products and brands purchased. Reference group concepts have long been used by advertisers in their efforts to persuade consumers to purchase products and brands by portraying products being consumed in socially attractive situations and using attractive people and getting prominent spokespersons to endorse products. This demonstrates the belief that reference groups have the ability to shape behavior, adopt certain lifestyles, influence self-concept and contribute to the formation of values and attitudes (Bearden and Etzel, 1982).

Bourne (1957) suggested that reference group influence on product and brand decisions is a function of two forms of "conspicuousness." Firstly, the item must be conspicuous in the sense that it can be seen and identified by public and secondly, the product must be exclusive which means that the product must not be owned by virtually everyone. A marketer must determine in which classification a product falls, but if neither the product nor brand appears to be associated with reference group influence, advertising should emphasize the product attributes, price, etc. Where reference group influence is operative, the advertiser should stress the kinds of people who buy the products (ibid).

Extending Bourne's framework, Bearden and Etzel (1982) investigated the three types of reference group influence on product and brand decisions. Item *"exclusivity"* was operationalized as luxuries and necessities whereas items *"seen or identified"* by others were operationalized as publicly and privately consumed products. Their study revealed that reference group influence is strong in publicly consumed necessities and luxuries. This was because these products were more conspicuous and thus, respondents were able to observe the products and brands purchased by referents or interact with referents regarding the appropriate products and brands to buy.

Childers and Rao (1992) studied the influence of familial and peer influence on consumer decisions in different cultural contexts and confirmed Bearden and Etzel's (1982) findings. Further, they found that for privately consumed goods, parental influence on brand decisions was higher because of the limited opportunity to observe the brand preferences of peers. Intergenerational influence on privately consumed products was higher for extended families than for nuclear families.

As discussed earlier, while product-choice and the reference group influence have received considerable attention in the area of tangible products, their influence in service-selection decisions is still in its early stages of development. Arora and Stoner (1995) extended the knowledge of reference group influence from tangible products to services and examined the three types of reference group influences—informational, utilitarian and value expressive. However, they did not make any distinction between services and brand decisions.

RATIONALE FOR RESEARCH

A review of literature revealed that studies addressing social influences in marketing have received limited attention. More so, most were conducted in the setting of product purchase and not of services. Furthermore, most studies (including Arora and Stoner, 1995) used students as respondents, raising a serious concern on the external validity (Park and Lessig, 1977) of the results. Hence, this study used working women in Singapore as subjects to allow wider generalizations.

WHY WORKING WOMEN?

In recent years, there has been a rising interest in the study of women because they are becoming prominent figures in the workplace. In the 1950s, US women only constituted 33.9% of the workplace, whereas in the 1990s, the figure surged to 45.6% (US Department of Labor, 1993). In Singapore too, there has been a similar trend of women entering the workforce. Between 1957 and 1994, female labor force participation jumped from 19.3% to 50.9%. Average monthly income from work for females too, rose significantly from $421 in 1980 to $1,584 in 1990, an increase of 276% (Singapore Census of Population, 1990). By 2000, it is predicted that women will form the majority of new entrants into the workforce. On the whole women, due to their increasing affluence, have considerable spending power and hence are a potential segment for local service providers to tap on.

WHY SINGAPORE?

In the past decade, Singapore has gone through tremendous economic growth. It has grown 400% faster than Australia (Paul, 1993) and has surpassed many developed countries, e.g., England, Canada, etc., in per capita GDP. In the last two and a half decades, its unemployment rate and inflation have decreased by more than two thirds, while its per capita GDP has increased a whopping 13 times. The World Bank (1995) has ranked Singapore as ninth among the richest countries of the world in terms of purchasing power parity. It is now considered a more advanced developing country (The Straits Times, 17 Jan 1996). Due to their high per capita income, Singaporeans are the focus of marketers in the region. Moreover, the transition from a developing country to a more advanced one brings about changes in outlook, viewpoints and expectations among the people, which is likely to affect the susceptibility to reference group influence of the consumers. Past research has focused on either developing or developed countries, but has rarely looked into intermediate ones. Research systematically investigating the effect of societal development on the reference group influence in a multiracial population will be of prime importance to both domestic and international marketers in terms of designing marketing strategies and promotional campaigns, etc. Further, many developing countries are trying to emulate Singapore's economic policies and are expected to be in the same position sooner or later. Hence the same strategies may be applied there too in the not so distant future.

PERCEIVED RISK

Researchers have examined the different types of perceived risks and risk-reducing strategies on a wide range of services, especially professional services and retailing. However, no attempt has been made to determine the types of risk among the two types of services differing in "conspicuousness." Bearden and Etzel (1982) pointed out that the distinction between luxuries and necessities implied varying costs and hence different degrees of risk. Bruce and Witt (1972) suggested seven determinants of the social influence process. These included perceived risk and perceived conspicuousness of the product or service. This points to an interesting area of research in perceived risks and conspicuousness of services.

This study intends to replicate and extend Arora and Stoner's research (1995) by assessing whether their findings stand the test of time and by exploring the relationship between types of perceived risks and service conspicuousness. Hence, this study will allow for an assessment of reference groups influence on working women for different services in Singapore. Secondly, it allows for the identification of risk dimensions that influence service decision making for different purchase situations.

SELECTION OF SERVICES

Two general guidelines were utilized while selecting specific services to represent each of the four categories of services to be examined. Firstly, the service must have a high level of awareness and usage. Awareness was conceptualized as a rudimentary level of knowledge about a brand of service that includes at least brand name recognition (Hoyer and Brown, 1990). Secondly, the selection of service requires the user to make a deliberate choice. Hence, fine dining restaurant and beauty care services were selected as publicly consumed luxuries and privately consumed luxury, while dental care services and haircut were selected to represent privately consumed necessity and publicly consumed necessity (Table 1).

Privately Consumed Luxuries are services that are consumed out of public view and are not commonly used by everyone. For products in this category, the brand is not socially important and is a matter of individual choice, but ownership of the product does convey a message about the owner (Bourne, 1957). Services consumed in public view but not commonly used fall in the publicly consumed luxuries category. Since the service is a luxury, reference group influence should be strong. Publicly Consumed Necessities are services which are observed in public when consumed and are used essentially by everybody. Thus, there is strong pressure to conform to social norms. Privately Consumed Necessities are services that are neither observable nor exclusive

TABLE 1. Services Considered in the Study

	Public	Private
Luxury	Fine dining restaurant	Beauty care services
Necessity	Haircut	Dental care services

because they are consumed out of public view and are used by everybody. Purchasing behavior of such services should be governed largely by service attributes rather than by influence of others (Bearden and Etzel, 1982).

A focus group study consisting of six respondents revealed that beauty care was a appropriate choice for privately consumed luxury because it has a high level of usage and awareness among the subjects of this study and because its purchasers are required to make a deliberate choice decision.

Since fine dining is expensive, it is not used by everyone. Thus, they are chosen as publicly consumed luxuries for this study, while haircut services are consumed by everyone and hence, they are considered as necessities. As in the case of fine dining restaurant, patrons of a hairdressing salon are physically exposed to the service personnel as well as other patrons of the salon when consuming the service. Also, haircut is a necessity and is easily seen by others during consumption, hence, it is considered to be a publicly consumed necessity. Beauty care services are carried out in the privacy of individual rooms but are not consumed by everyone and hence, they fall in the privately consumed category. Dental care services are considered as privately consumed necessities as this service is consumed by almost everyone and the treatment is carried out in the privacy of individual rooms.

RESEARCH HYPOTHESES

The social visibility and exclusivity factors associated with publicly consumed luxuries suggests that they will be more susceptible to normative (utilitarian and value-expressive) reference group influence than the less conspicuous privately consumed luxuries (Childers and Rao, 1992). Specifically, the visibility factor provides considerations for perceived social approval or disapproval as well as rewards and punishments. Thus, utilitarian influence should be significant in this relationship. Furthermore, the conspicuous consumption of the service suggests that there may be a strong incentive for image enhancement and hence, the individual's self-concept. Thus, value-expressive influence should also be significant in this relationship. Hence, we propose that:

H1: *Utilitarian and value-expressive reference group influences are higher for publicly consumed luxuries (fine dining restaurant) than for privately consumed luxuries (beauty care services).*

In addition, as both services are luxuries and hence, not commonly used, consumers may acquire information from external sources to make informed decisions. Hence no difference in informational reference group influence is expected.

H2:   *There will be no difference in informational reference group influence between publicly consumed luxuries (fine dining restaurant) and privately consumed luxuries (beauty care services).*

The relative exclusivity of luxury services implies that informational reference group influence will be higher for them than for necessity services. Also, the considerations of social approval and gain of rewards from others are more compelling for luxury services than for necessity services. For example, patronizing a fine dining restaurant reflects social importance (June and Smith, 1993) and the consumer seeks personal sources of information regarding the choice of a restaurant (Sweeney, Johnson and Armstrong, 1992).

H3:   *All three forms of reference group influences are higher for publicly consumed luxuries (fine dining) than publicly consumed necessities (haircut).*

As publicly consumed necessities are consumed in public view and are used by virtually everyone, little informational influence is expected. There is also strong pressure to conform (Arora and Stoner, 1995). Further, since the service chosen for this category is haircut where the outcome (i.e., the new hairdo) is visible to others, style and appearance are affected by personal perceptions. The respondents are also able to observe the hairdos of others and to interact with them regarding the reliability of the service provider. Thus, utilitarian influence is more significant than informational and value expressive influence.

H4:   *For publicly consumed necessities (hair cut), Utilitarian reference group influence is higher than informational and value-expressive reference group influences.*

Privately Consumed Necessities are not consumed in the presence of others and yet are consumed by almost everyone. Thus, there is little opportunity for image enhancement and hence, self-concept. Further, the inconspicuous nature of consumption and unknown consequences of service consumption to others may not encourage consumers to interact with others regarding the service provider. Therefore, there is little pressure to conform with the reference group. However, consumers are still expected to obtain information about the service due to the high perceived risk.

H5:   *For privately consumed necessities (dental services), informational reference group influence is higher than utilitarian and value-expressive reference group influences.*

Since privately consumed luxuries are services whose consumption is not observed by others and to a large extent are exclusive, utilitarian and value-expressive influences are not significant in these services because there is little need for image enhancement and pressure to conform. The private consumption of the service also does not allow observation of the service provider patronized.

H6: *Informational reference group influence is higher than utilitarian and value-expressive reference group influences for privately consumed luxuries (beauty care services).*

RESEARCH METHOD

For the first objective, a 3 (type of reference group influence) $\times$ 2 (public versus private) $\times$ 2 (luxury versus necessity) within subjects factorial design was utilized to determine the nature of reference group influence in the four services. The second objective was to determine the perceived risk dimensions for each of the four services. Thus, a 6 (types of perceived losses) $\times$ 2 (public versus private) $\times$ 2 (necessity versus luxury) within subjects factorial design was used.

Reference group influence for each service was assessed using 10 items; the three variations of group influence were represented as a summed composite of four informational, two utilitarian and four value-expressive items. All the items were made up of a seven point Likert type scale ranging from strongly disagree to strongly agree.

The items used for this study were adopted from Arora and Stoner's (1995) research, who in turn selected them from an extensive review of the literature (Bearden and Etzel, 1982; Netemeyer and Teel, 1989; Childers and Rao, 1992). Some modifications to the items were made to adequately capture the concepts in the local context, e.g., an informational influence item referring to opinion of food critics was omitted because such reviews are published in the media every week (*The Sunday Times–Sunday Plus!* under Leisure section) and thus, overlapped with one of the items which referred to influence by reviews in media. Instead, a statement referring to reliable information provided by one's family members, friends and colleagues was adopted from Park and Lessig's (1977) list of items.

In the context of the restaurant, items for informational reference group influence included "I seek the opinions of people who work in restaurants," "I seek the opinions of friends, family members, relatives and colleagues who have reliable information about different restaurants," and "I use the restaurant reviews from media (e.g., *The Business's Guide to Entertainment*) to guide my selection of a restaurant." In the same context (fine dining restaurant), examples of Utilitarian Reference Group Influence included "I observe the choices of restaurants made by experts," and "My selection of a restaurant is influenced by my friend's, colleague's and family member's preferences towards the restaurant," while examples of Value-Expressive Reference Group Influence included "I feel that people who dine at a particular restaurant are admired or respected by others," and "I feel that the people who dine at a particular restaurant possess the characteristics which I would like to have."

Six items were used to measure the probability of the six types of losses from the purchase of the four services (see Table 2). The risks included were financial risk, social risk, physical risk, performance risk, time risk and psychological risk. The items were selected and adapted after an extensive review of the literature (Mitchell and Greatorex, 1993; Garner, 1986). The individual items were operationalized as one-item seven-point Likert type scales ranging from strongly disagree to strongly agree. Scales were scored so that higher values represented greater risk perception.

Data Collection

Data were collected using a self-administered questionnaires distributed to the subjects using representative sampling method by geographical location and time of the day. Before the questionnaires were distributed, it was made sure that the respondents were familiar with all the services in the study and had consumed them at least once in the last three months.

The questionnaire comprised of three sections. Questions in section I were designed to measure reference group influence; section II measured different

TABLE 2. Items Used to Measure the Various Types of Perceived Risk

Financial Risk	Social Risk	Physical Risk	Performance Risk	Time Risk	Psychological Risk
I am concerned that the use of a particular restaurant will lead to loss of money for me as a result of the service failing such as poor service, food and/or environment.	I am concerned that the use of a particular restaurant will lead to embarrassment for me if my friends, colleagues and family know that the service has failed.	I am concerned that the use of a particular restaurant will pose as a physical hazard (health) to me as a result of the service failing.	I am concerned that a particular restaurant will not provide the level of customer satisfaction that I had expected.	I am concerned that the use of a particular restaurant will lead to time loss as a result of time necessary to rectify the failure, mistakes, errors such as wrong food served.	I am concerned that the use of a particular restaurant will lead to loss of self-esteem if my friends, colleagues and family know that the service has failed.

types of perceived losses, whereas section III probed into demographic characteristics of respondents. It was ensured that the respondents were familiar with all four services and had consumed them before.

Out of a total of 270 questionnaires given out, 150 were returned, thus generating a response rate of 57.8%. Eighty percent of the respondents were in the age group of 20-39 years old. Fifty-two percent of them earned a monthly income of $2,000 and below. Married respondents formed about 37% of the total sample. Generally, the respondents were highly educated, with 39% receiving university education.

The Cronbach alpha value for all the three types of reference group influence for the four services were beyond the acceptable level of 0.70 indicating that the scales were reliable (Nunnally, 1978). A factor analysis with principal component analysis and varimax rotation revealed that fine dining restaurant and dental care services had similar factor loadings whereas beauty care services and haircut were loaded in another similar manner (only statements with factor loadings of at least 0.50 were included). This could partially be explained by the unique nature of the services chosen; while the consequences of a meal at a fine dining restaurant and a visit to the dentist are not socially visible, a new hairdo or tattooed eyebrow are undeniably socially visible.

In the case of fine dining restaurant and dental care services, the items were loaded on three factors. The first factor, termed "seeking information from outside sources" suggested the importance of outside sources of information, e.g., the media and the message transmitted. The second factor, termed "gaining information and approval from personal sources" suggested that the consumer strongly valued information provided by her friends, family members and colleagues. This is especially common in Asian societies where consumers are less individualistic and adhere more to social norms. Their closely-knit family structure and ties may also contribute to explaining this factor. The third factor termed "seeking information from others to enhance one's self-image" suggested the importance of image enhancement.

The items for beauty care services and haircut loaded heavily on two factors only (see Table 3). The first factor was also termed "gaining information and approval from personal sources." It must be highlighted that "seeking information from experts" also fell into this category. The second factor was termed "seeking information or observing behavior of others to enhance one's self-image."

Reference Group Influence Across Services

The analysis revealed that respondents rated the fine dining restaurant highest for all three types of reference group influences. A posteriori multiple comparison of mean scores for each type of reference group influence for the four services through the Scheffe method revealed that utilitarian reference group influence was significantly higher for fine dining restaurant than for beauty care services ($\alpha = 0.05$). However, the results failed to support the hypothesis that value expressive reference group influence for fine dining restaurant was higher than beauty care services ($\alpha = 0.05$). Hence, the first hypothesis was partially supported.

Results also suggested that there was no significant difference between informational reference group influence in the case of fine dining restaurant (publicly consumed luxury) and beauty care services (privately consumed luxury) (Table 4). Hence, H2 is supported.

The ANOVA results also showed that informational and utilitarian influences for fine dining restaurant were significantly higher than haircut services ($\alpha = 0.05$). However, the results did not support differences for value expressive reference group influence for both the services ($\alpha = 0.05$). Hence, H3 is

TABLE 3. Comparison of Reference Group Influence Across the Four Services

Reference Group Influence	Services				
	Fine Dining Restaurant	Beauty Care Services	Haircut	Dental Care Services	Significance[1]
Informational	4.7844	4.4810	4.3800	4.4889	0.0159*
Utilitarian	4.4233	3.9128	3.8367	3.7233	0.0004*
Value Expressive	2.9400	2.8389	2.8600	2.4183	0.0015*
Significance[2]	0.0000*	0.0000*	0.0000*	0.0000*	

[1] Significance of reference group influence across services
[2] Significance of various types of reference group influence within a service

TABLE 4. One-Way Analysis of Variance Among Services on Reference Group Influence

Type of Reference Group Influence	Mean Reference Group Influence				
	Fine Dining Restaurant (Group 1)	Beauty Care Service (Group 2)	Haircut (Group 3)	Dental Care Services (Group 4)	Posteriori Test (Scheffe) *
Informational	4.7844	4.4810	4.3800	4.4889	1 & 3
Utilitarian	4.4233	3.9128	3.9128	3.7233	1 & 2, 1 & 3, 1 & 4
Value Expressive	2.9400	2.8389	2.8600	2.4183	1 & 4, 2 & 4, 3 & 4

* Both groups are significantly different at $\alpha = 0.05$

not supported. This could mean that value expressive influence demonstrated similar effects on publicly consumed services. Also, the magnitude of informational and utilitarian reference group influence was higher for fine dining restaurant than for haircut, indicating that they were more powerful in determining the choice of fine dining restaurants.

Reference Group Influence Within Services

Within each of the four services, informational influence seemed to be the dominant factor among the three types of reference group influence, whereas value expressive influence was the least dominant (Table 5). This seemed to imply a greater role for appeals based on informational reference group influence in stimulating demand for services.

Dental care services scored lowest for both utilitarian and value expressive reference group influences among the four services. However, it ranked second for informational reference group influence, falling behind fine dining restaurant. This implied that for dental care services, informational reference group influence may be more powerful source of influence than utilitarian and value expressive reference group influences.

Results also showed that for publicly consumed services (haircut and fine dining restaurant), utilitarian influence was significantly higher than value expressive influence ($\alpha = 0.05$). However, utilitarian influence was less than informational influence, thus negating the second part of the hypothesis. Accordingly, the fourth hypothesis was partially supported.

TABLE 5. One-Way Analysis of Variance Among Reference Group Influences on Services

Services	Means			
	Informational Reference Group Influence (Group 1)	Utilitarian Reference Group Influence (Group 2)	Value Expressive Group Influence (Group 3)	Posteriori Test (Scheffe)*
Fine Dining Restaurant	4.7844	4.4233	2.9400	1 & 2, 1 & 3, 2 & 3
Beauty Care Services	4.4810	3.9128	2.8600	1 & 2, 1& 3, 2 & 3
Haircut	4.3800	3.9128	2.8600	1 & 3, 2 & 3, 1 & 2
Dental Care Services	4.4889	3.7233	2.4183	1 & 2, 1 & 3, 2 & 3

* Both groups are significantly different at $\alpha = 0.05$

The analysis suggested that for dental care services, informational influence was stronger than utilitarian and value expressive influences ($a = 0.05$). Hence, H5 is supported. It was also observed that for privately consumed luxuries (beauty care services) informational influence was stronger than utilitarian and value expressive reference group influences ($\alpha = 0.05$). Hence, H6 is also supported.

Comparison of Reference Group Influence Across Services

In general, the study revealed greater utilitarian and informational reference group influence for publicly consumed luxuries than for privately consumed luxuries. The visibility factor suggests that social approval was a reasonable considerations. However, value expressive reference group influence demonstrated similar effects on both the luxury services. This could partially be explained by the nature of beauty care services and fine dining restaurant. In general, women are more concerned about looking good and may want to adopt the service provider patronized by a referent whom they admire or like, such as famous celebrity endorsers for beauty salons to enhance their self-image and concept.

Both informational and utilitarian reference group influences were greater for publicly consumed luxury (fine dining restaurant) than for publicly consumed necessity (haircut). It is quite logical that consumer information needs and desire for social approval would be greater for luxury services than for necessity services. This is consistent with previous research that personal sources of information from friends and relatives influence the restaurant selection decision (Sweeney, Johnson and Armstrong, 1992). Another reason is that although beauty care services were chosen as privately consumed luxuries in this study, the results were socially visible (e.g., tattooed eyebrows). Hence, the need for social approval.

When considering publicly consumed necessities, informational reference group influence demonstrated a greater impact than did utilitarian and value expressive influence. This showed the respondent's greater willingness to acquire reliable information about these services. However, as the magnitude of utilitarian reference group influence was reasonably high, service providers should not solely focus on informational, but also on value expressive reference group influence.

As hypothesized, for privately consumed necessities, informational reference group influence was more powerful in affecting service choice than utilitarian and value expressive influences. Since these services have low social visibility and exclusivity, there seems to be less need for image enhancement and social approval. Hence the low utilitarian and value expressive influence on service purchase decisions.

For privately consumed luxuries, informational influence was stronger than utilitarian and value expressive influences. While the privacy of this service usage would suggest that this decision has little utilitarian and value expressive impact, the magnitude for utilitarian and value expressive reference group influence was rather high. These findings may be due to the visible consequences of the specific service chosen for this study (beauty care services). Thus, there was pressure for the respondents to conform to social norms and enhance one's self image.

Analysis of Perceived Risks of Services

The second objective of the study was to analyze and rank the six types of perceived risks associated with the consumption of the four services. Overall risk for each service was obtained by summing up the six types of risks (Table 6).

Beauty care services were seen to have the highest level of total perceived risk whereas fine dining restaurant, the lowest. Further, both beauty care services and haircut had relatively higher scores for social, psychological and time risks than the other two services. Mitchell and Greatorex (1993) noted that haircut carried a very high risk because of its psychosocial consequences. This could be explained by the socially visible nature of a haircut and beauty care services such as a new hairdo or tattooed eyebrows. Moreover, it was also observed that both beauty care services and haircut had almost similar ratings for all types of perceived risks and hence had similar rankings.

On the other hand, it appeared that financial and performance risks were the most important when choosing a fine dining restaurant. Mitchell and Greatorex (1993) too found that financial loss was the most important consideration in

TABLE 6. Mean Perceived Risk for the Four Different Services

Service	Means						
	Financial Risk	Social Risk	Physical Risk	Psychological Risk	Time Risk	Performance Risk	Total Risk
Fine Dining Restaurant	5.1667 (1)*	4.1133 (4)	3.9733 (5)	3.7600 (6)	4.2333 (3)	4.7600 (2)	26.007
Beauty Care Services	5.0403 (4)	5.6467 (1)	4.3333 (5)	5.6000 (2)	5.4800 (3)	4.1812 (6)	30.282
Haircut	4.9732 (4)	5.6000 (1)	4.4733 (5)	5.5867 (2)	5.3400 (3)	4.1477 (6)	30.121
Dental Care Services	4.4267 (4)	4.0067 (5)	5.2533 (1)	3.1333 (6)	4.9267 (2)	4.9200 (3)	26.667

*Numbers in parentheses are rankings of perceived risks within each service

the selection of a restaurant. Performance risk was found to be high because of the difficulty in evaluating a restaurant's performance prior to consumption.

Dental care services were perceived to have high physical and time risks. Garner and Garner (1985) too, found that time loss was important in the purchase of physician services. Most dental consultations take place during office hours, which meant that the respondents might have to apply for time or day off from work to visit the dentist. Moreover, the waiting time at these places could sometimes be quite high. On the other hand, physical risk was featured greatly for dental care services because of the pain associated with it.

Perceived Risk and Service Conspicuousness

The ANOVA showed that physical risk was significantly higher for necessity services than for luxury services (Table 7). This could be largely due to the unique nature of dental care services where consumers were more concerned about pain or other health hazard in case something went wrong. Financial risk was found to have a greater effect on luxury items than for necessity items. This finding too, seemed logical due to the relatively higher costs of luxury services. Psychological risk too was also found to be higher for luxury services than for necessity services. Thus, it was felt that status and image implications were more important for luxury services than for necessity services. After spending high amounts of money, people expect luxury services to perform well.

Results also suggested that time risk was greater for privately consumed services (beauty care and dental services) than for publicly consumed services (fine dining restaurant and haircut). This suggests that such service providers

TABLE 7. Perceived Risk for the Four Services

Type of perceived risk	Necessity services (haircut and dental care)	Luxury services (fine dining restaurant and beauty care)	p	Publicly Consumed Services (fine dining restaurant and haircut)	Privately Consumed Services (beauty care services and dental care)	p
Social risk	4.81	4.703	0.309	4.68	4.83	0.193
Physical risk	4.55	3.82	0.000*	3.91	4.46	0.000*
Performance risk	4.56	4.52	0.740	4.49	4.59	0.430
Financial risk	4.70	5.05	0.047*	5.06	4.67	0.027*
Time risk	4.87	4.53	0.064	4.47	4.87	0.010*
Psychological risk	4.433	4.683	0.029*	4.747	4.370	0.001*

* significant at $\alpha = 0.05$

should try to reduce the time involved in delivering the service (e.g., waiting time). Lastly, psychological risk was found to be significantly higher for publicly consumed services than for privately consumed services. The conspicuous nature of the former suggested a strong incentive for image enhancement.

DISCUSSIONS AND IMPLICATIONS

The findings in this study indicate that informational reference group influence has the most influential impact on all four services, more so for luxury services (see Table 8). This sends a powerful message that service marketers should focus primarily on informational reference group in their communication efforts. One form of informational reference group influence is word-of-mouth (WOM). It has been estimated that as much as eighty per cent of all buying decisions were influenced by someone's direct recommendations (Voss, 1984). Marketers should be attentive to the existing WOM activity in the market place and try to adjust their marketing efforts to generate positive WOM. This is all the more pertinent in the case of services as they are difficult to be evaluated prior to purchase and thus, any information provided by friends, relatives and colleagues is valued strongly. Marketers should also provide quality service and/or products to stimulate positive WOM. Further, service establishments should pay heed to customer feedback/complaints and act promptly.

In another aspect, marketers can also generate informational reference group influence through the use of experts and professionals. For example, marketers of fine-dining restaurants could invite connoisseurs to do a write up in the media such as *The Business Guide to Entertainment*. This could prove to be a credible source of information to businessmen who need to entertain guests frequently but do not have the time to spend on information search. In addition, restaurants can hire connoisseurs to recommend their restaurants to the TV audience. This would prove to be effective since they are the experts in delicacies. The importance of informational reference group influence may

TABLE 8. Summary of Reference Group Influence

Types of Reference Group Influence	Fine Dining Restaurant	Beauty Care Services	Haircut	Dental Care Services
Informational	high	high	high	high
Utilitarian	high	moderate-high	moderate-high	moderate
Value Expressive	low-moderate	low-moderate	low-moderate	low

also affect the choice of spokespersons and their message in advertisements. Accordingly, presenting a message that focuses on knowledge, expertise and credibility should be preferred.

Utilitarian influence is also found to strongly affect consumer's choice of luxury services as well as service's whose results are highly socially visible. Thus, the preferences of friends, family members and colleagues become critical in the selection process of these services. For example, in the case of restaurants, the considerations of social approval and disapproval are compelling because they affect the pleasure and enjoyment during the meal. For services where the results are socially visible (e.g., a haircut), it is important for marketers to realize the consumer's need to conform to social pressure so as to be socially accepted. Thus, presenting an affective message which suggests that their services are regularly used by referents may prove to be effective. In addition, promotions such as discounts to patrons when they bring a friend along may be successful in generating additional demand.

Value expressive reference group influence was found to be high for publicly consumed services. This signals that marketers should focus on image enhancement. Thus, messages that are emotionally charged may be preferred. For example, Citibank's preferred card advertisement portrays the exclusive lifestyle of the rich which most people aspire to have. It indirectly enhances the self-image of consumers through the concept of referent identification by transmitting the message that they too could enjoy that kind of lifestyle if they sign up with Citibank.

Generally, there is no one distinct reference group influence to follow for any service. It may require a combination of the different types of reference group influence with varying degrees of usage. For instance in the case of beauty care services which is greatly influenced by all three types of reference group influence, marketers could address some of the needs by providing factual information about their services and products as well as showing its "success stories" on celebrities.

It is essential for managers to understand the manner in which consumers form perceptions of risk for service purchases. Due to the inherent differences in the perceived risk associated with services, different types of risk reducing strategies are necessary.

For luxury services, financial and psychological risks were considered important. Although financial risk is difficult for managers to deal with since prices are influenced by a number of factors including costs, quality perceptions etc., providing discount coupons or offering guarantees can be effective strategies for reducing uncertainties associated with financial risk. Psychological risk can be reduced by WOM from friends, family members and colleagues. Marketers could also discuss the quality of their service in the media by using real life spokespersons or celebrities to speak about their experiences with the service. This could reduce the amount of psychological risk associated with the purchase of luxury services. This strategy also applies to publicly consumed services which are also high in psychological risk. Finally, for privately consumed services, the presence of time loss indicates the need for a more efficient booking system, service guarantees and emphasizing employee training to standardize service delivery.

Limitations of the Study and Directions for Future Research

Firstly, this study is limited by the omission of variables such as familiarity of services, stages in decision making and individual attributes such as personal level of self-confidence. Susceptibility to influence by others is also related to other personal characteristics, e.g., self-esteem and intelligence (McGuire, 1968; Petty and Cacioppo, 1981). However, it was not possible to include all these personal attributes into this study due to time and length constraints.

In general, results indicated that working women in Singapore were subject to high informational reference group influence followed by utilitarian and value-expressive reference group influences, respectively. This could be due to a peculiar characteristic of working women. Future research should systematically investigate the reasons for this finding and whether working men, too, behave similarly.

The study was limited to working women and may not be representative of the population at large. It also limited to women who were literate and those who understood English. Future researchers should attempt to overcome these limitations and study reference group influence in other groups of the population and different populations and cultures and further our understanding of the area.

REFERENCES

Anonymous, (1996), *Singapore, 1965-1995 Statistical Highlights: A Review of 30 Years' Development,* Department of Statistics, Singapore.

Arora, Raj and Stoner, Charles (1995), "Reference Group Influence on Selection of Services," *Journal of Customer Service in Marketing and Management,* 1 (3) pp. 79-93.

Asch, S. (1953), "Effects of Group Pressure upon the Modification and Distortion of Judgments," in *Readings in Social Psychology,* New York: Holt, Rhinehart & Winston, pp. 174-182.

Bateson, J. E. G. (1995), *Managing Services Marketing: Text and Readings,* 3rd Edition, Fortworth: The Dryden Press p. 680.

Bauer, R. A. (1960), "Consumer Behavior as Risk Taking" in *Dynamic Marketing for a Changing World,* R.S. Hancock (ed.), Chicago, AMA Proceedings p. 24.

Bearden, William O. and Etzel, Michael J. (1982), "Reference Group Influence on Product and Brand-Purchase Decisions," *Journal of Consumer Research*, 9 (September), pp. 183-193.

Childers, Terry L. and Rao, Akshay R. (1992), "The Influence of Familial and Peer-based Reference Groups on Consumer Decisions," *Journal of Consumer Research*, 19 (September) pp. 198-211.

Deutsch, M. and Gerard, H. (1955), "A Study of Normative and Informative Social Influences Upon Individual Judgment," *Journal of Abnormal and Social Psychology*, 51 pp. 629-636.

Garner, S. J. (1986), "Perceived Risk and Information Search in Services Purchasing," *Mid-Atlantic Journal of Business*, 16 (2) pp. 19-25.

Guseman, D. S. (1981), "Risk Perception and Risk Reduction in Consumer Services," in *Proceedings of the American Marketing Association*, J. M. Donnely and W. R. George (eds.) pp. 200-204.

June, Leslie P. and Smith, Stephen L. J. (1987), "Service Attributes and Situational Effects on Customer Preferences for Restaurant Dining," *Journal of Travel Research*, 25 (3, Fall) pp. 20-27.

Lovelock, Christopher L. (1981), "Why Marketing Management Needs to be Different for Services," in *Marketing of Services*, James H. Donnelly and William R. George (eds.), Chicago: American Marketing Association, pp. 5-9.

Lisko M. (1983), *"The Road Race: An Untapped Promotional Tool,"* in *Marketing Theories and Concepts from an Era of Change*, J. Summey et al. (eds.), Chicago: AMA.

Mitchell, V. W and Greatorex, M. (1993), "Risk Perception and Reduction in the Purchase of Consumer Services," *The Services Industries Journal*, 13 (4) pp 179-200.

Nunnally, J. C. (1978), *Psychometric Theory*, 2nd edition, New York: McGraw Hill.

Park, C. Whan and Lessig, Parker V. (1977), "Students and Housewives: Differences in Susceptibility to Reference Group Influence," *Journal of Consumer Research*, 4 (September) pp. 102-109.

Perry, Michael and Hamm, B. Curtis (1969), "Canonical Analysis of Relations behveen Socioeconomic Risk and Personal Influence in Purchase Decisions," *Journal of Marketing Research*, 6 (August) pp. 351-354.

Price, Linda L., and Feick, Lawrence L. (1984), "The Role of Interpersonal Sources in External Search: An Informational Perspective," in *Advances in Consumer Research*, Vol. 11, Thomas C. Kinnear (ed), Provo, UT: Association for Consumer Research pp. 250-255.

Sheth, J. N. (1974), "A Theory of Family Buying Decisions" In: *Models of Buyer Behavior: Conceptual Quantitative and Empirical*, J. N. Sheth (ed.), Harper & Row, New York, pp. 17-33.

Sherif, Muzafer (1935), "A Study of Some Social Factors in Perception," *Archives of Psychology*, 27 (187) pp. 60.

Sweeney, Jillian C., Johnson, Lester W. and Armstrong, Robert W. (1992), "The Effects of Cues on Service Quality Expectations and Service Selection in a Restaurant Setting," *Journal of Services Marketing*, 6 (4, Fall) pp. 15-22.

Turley, L. W. and Leblanc, Ronald P. (1993), "An Exploratory Investigation of Consumer Decision Making in the Service Sector," *Journal of Services Marketing*, 7 (4) pp. 11-18.

Venkatesan, M. (1966), "Experimental Study of Consumer Behavior Conformity and Independence," *Journal of Marketing Research*, (November), pp. 473-78.

Voss, P. Jr. (1984), "Status shifts to peer influence," *Advertising Age*, (17 May), pp. 1-10.

Witt, Robert E.and Bruce, Grady D. (1972), "Group Influence and Brand Choice Congnience," *Journal of Marketing Research*, 8 (November) pp. 440-443.

Emotional Influences of Environmental Cues on Chinese Consumers in a Leisure Service Setting

Esther P. Y. Tang
Ricky Y. K. Chan
Susan H. C. Tai

SUMMARY. This study investigates the emotional influence of environmental cues on Chinese consumers under a leisure service setting. By surveying 200 Chinese customers of game centers in Guangzhou, China, empirical findings of this study confirm the belief that the perceived physical environment of the game center exerts a direct and positive influence on Chinese customers' emotional state as well as on their repatronge intention. They also indicate that if such an environment really makes customers feel excited, their excitement will, in turn, induce them to spend more resources in the center. Despite the fact that many researchers have suggested that Chinese consumers may adopt unique consumption characteristics, the influence of physical environment of a service setting on consumer responses seems to remain intact in both

---

Esther P.Y. Tang and Ricky Y.K. Chan are Associate Professors, and Susan H.C. Tai is Assistant Professor, all at the Department of Business, Hong Kong, Polytechnic University.

Address correspondence to: Esther P.Y. Tang, Department of Business Studies, The Hong Kong Polytechnic University, Kowloon, Hong Kong (E-mail: buesther@polyu. edu.hk).

[Haworth co-indexing entry note]: "Emotional Influences of Environmental Cues on Chinese Consumers in a Leisure Service Setting." Tang, Esther P. Y., Ricky Y. K. Chan, and Susan H. C. Tai. Co-published simultaneously in *Journal of International Consumer Marketing* (International Business Press, an imprint of The Haworth Press, Inc.) Vol. 14, No. 1, 2001, pp. 67-87; and: *Asian Dimensions of Services Marketing* (ed: Esther P. Y. Tang, Ricky Y. K. Chan, and Susan H. C. Tai) International Business Press, an imprint of The Haworth Press, Inc., 2001, pp. 67-87. Single or multiple copies of this article are available for a fee from The Haworth Document Delivery Service [1-800-342-9678, 9:00 a.m. - 5:00 p.m. (EST). E-mail address: getinfo@ haworthpressinc.com].

67

Western and Chinese cultures. These findings remind service executives operating in Chinese societies of the importance to pay close attention to all aspects of their service environment to ensure corporate success. Lastly, the lack of a significant relationship between resource expenditure and repatronage intention identified in this study also warrants further exploration in future research. *[Article copies available for a fee from The Haworth Document Delivery Service: 1-800-342-9678. E-mail address: <getinfo@haworthpressinc.com> Website: <http://www.HaworthPress.com> © 2001 by The Haworth Press, Inc. All rights reserved.]*

KEYWORDS. Environmental cue, leisure service, Chinese emotion

INTRODUCTION

Shopping is becoming less and less about acquisition and more and more about experience. Ice rinks, cinemas, and game complexes are in the business of selling experience and their success has led to the creation of retail centers that rely more on entertainment than merchandise for their success (McCloud, 1999). Recent research in services has recognized the experiential nature of services and that the emotional state of consumers during consumption has increasingly attracted attention from marketing researchers (Wirtz and Bateson, 1999; Herrington and Capella, 1996; Darden and Babin, 1994; Bitner, 1992).

While many past studies have been devoted to examining the effects of the physical environment on consumer emotions at the store or mall level, such examination in the setting of a leisure center is much rarer. In leisure service settings such as amusement parks, game centers, recreation clubs and resorts, excitement is often an end goal of consumers. An attractively designed physical environment can have a positive influence on consumers' feelings about the place. It has been advocated that consumers of leisure services would place more emphasis on pursuing pleasure or emotional fulfillment than functional usefulness from their service experience (Babin et al., 1994; Wakefield and Blodgett, 1994). Consumers' emotional responses to service environments are directly related to their willingness to spend time and money, and to browse, evaluate, and consume there (Donovan et al., 1994). Therefore a deeper understanding of how leisure center visitors really respond to emotion-provoked environmental cues should be of particular significance to practitioners. Specifically, such an understanding would be able to assist leisure center executives to develop more effective ways of shaping pre-visit and in-store emotions so as to enhance customer's desirability to revisit the center (Gardner, 1985; Wakefield and Bush, 1998).

Against this backdrop, the major objective of the present study is to empirically explore the relationships among environmental cues, customers' in-store emotions, customers' in-store resource expenditure and customer's repatronage intention in a selected leisure service setting–in this case, a game center.

RATIONALE AND THE SCOPE OF THE STUDY

For the present research, the scene is set at the entertainment game centers in China. A game center is characterized as a leisure service setting where customers are mainly involved in hedonic consumption during a relatively short visit (Wakefield and Blodgett, 1999). These characteristics of the chosen setting enhance the practical significance of the present study, as how to maximize emotional impact through the tactful use of environmental cues during customer's limited period of stay becomes a pressing operational issue. In order to accomplish the foregoing research objective, this study has proposed a conceptual model and employed the structural equation modeling technique to verify it.

The use of Chinese shoppers as the subjects of investigation further contributes to the literature. Although a large volume of the extant literature (e.g., Donovan and Rossiter, 1982; Ridgway et al., 1994) has been devoted to studying the effect of in-store environmental stimuli on Western consumers' shopping emotions, little work of similar nature has been done in a Chinese cultural context (e.g., Tai and Fung 1997).

Moreover, it is generally agreed that Chinese emotional behavior provides an interesting contrast to Western emotional behavior (Russell and Michelle, 1996). Many writers on emotions argue that what appears to be the "same" antecedent event need not be the same psychologically. It can be construed differently by different people or at different times or places. Cultural differences in the antecedents of emotion might therefore suggest differences in how an event is construed, and differences in how an event is construed might consequently lead to cultural differences in emotional reactions to that event (Russell and Michelle, 1996). When considering Chinese cultural characteristics along with the issues under investigation, the same argument seems to apply too. To illustrate, it is worth noting that systematic research has indicated that Chinese people are, in general, less impulsive and excitable than their Western counterparts (Yang, 1993). Given this cultural difference, it is probable that the Chinese may not react to the emotion-induced environmental cues in the same way as Westerners. The possible differences in Chinese consumers' emotional responses further warrant the conduct of the present study.

Lastly, given China's rapid economic development, an investigation of how Chinese consumers emotionally react to environmental cues in a leisure service setting seems a timely topic. As it was observed above, the leisure service industry, which originated in the West, has been growing rapidly in China, and more and more Chinese citizens are seen to spend their leisure time inside such entertainment facilities as game centers, cinemas, and shopping malls. The China government's decision to reduce the workweek to five days has further freed urban workers and their families for more leisure activities (Cui, 1997). Along with China's continued economic growth, it is also noted that the younger and better-educated Chinese are commanding much higher salaries than their parents, thereby enabling them to adopt Western goods and amenities more readily (Cui, 1997; Li, 1997). According to a recent estimate, there are currently around fifty to seventy million such middle-class citizens in China who can afford a more leisurely and enjoyable lifestyle (*Apple Daily,* 26 October 2000). These lucrative potential customers of various leisure services pose both challenges and opportunities to leisure service managers. Hopefully, the findings from this study will provide practitioners with some valuable insights into meeting the challenges and capitalizing on the emerging business opportunities.

THE ENVIRONMENT-EMOTION BEHAVIOR FRAMEWORK

Many attempts to explain the effects of physical surroundings on people are based on research in environmental psychology. Mehrabian and Russell (1974) suggest that individuals respond emotionally to environmental stimuli that in turn lead to "approach-avoidance" behavior (Figure 1). Different emotional states are measured on dimensions such as degree of arousal (that is, amount of stimulation or excitement) and the pleasure-displeasure continuum. Emotional response measured on these dimensions can predict behaviors with respect to the environment. Consumers' approach-avoidance behavior in service environments includes how much they spend and how long they stay during that visit, as well as whether they would repatronize the same service environment in the future.

Russell and Pratt (1980) also depict individual responses to the physical surroundings as a set of emotions based on degrees of pleasant/unpleasant and

FIGURE 1. Model of Human-Environmental Interaction

Environmental Stimuli: Sights Sounds Temperature, etc.	→	Emotional response: Pleasure Arousal Dominance	→	Approach/Avoidance: Spending Patronage Attitudes

Adapted from Mehrabian and Russell (1974)

arousing/sleepy affective qualities. Combinations of pleasure and arousal result in excitement, whereas combinations of arousing and unpleasant feelings result in distress. When examining the emotional influences of environmental cues, one should note that the notion of how an individual actually perceives environmental cues would be more important than the objective "being" of the environmental cues themselves. Indeed, in the management literature, it has long been contended that it is not the external reality, but the way an individual thinks about reality that determines his behavioral responses (e.g., Miller, 1988).

A review of the marketing literature dealing with the effects of the physical surroundings on consumers (e.g., Babin and Darden, 1995; Bitner, 1992; Wakefield and Baker, 1998; Wakefield and Blodgett, 1996, 1999) shows that there are empirical evidence to support the major hypotheses proposed by Mehrabian and Russell (1974). Furthermore, it has been advocated that consumers of leisure services would place more emphasis on pursuing pleasure or emotional fulfillment than functional usefulness from their service experience (Babin et al., 1994; Wakefield and Blodgett, 1994).

POSSIBLE EMOTIONAL RESPONSES OF CHINESE SHOPPERS

In a Chinese cultural context, some may raise concern about whether the aforementioned Environment-Emotion-Behavior framework is still applicable. Their concern mainly revolves around a unique temperamental characteristic of the Chinese, namely low impulsivity.

In the field of psychology, several early commentators (e.g., Cheng, 1946; Hsu, 1949; Tseng, 1973) have long pointed out that Chinese people have a lower degree of impulsivity than American people. When judged along with Kluckhohn and Strodtbeck's (1961) notion of cultural values, it is likely that the relative lower impulsivity of the Chinese is attributed to their unique "personal activity" orientation. Consistent with this, Yau (1994) further advocates that Chinese people have long been influenced by a system of semi-formal norms of behavior prescribed by Confucian teachings, called *Li*. This system prescribes the way the Chinese should or should not behave in order to maintain social harmony with other members of society. The observance of *Li* further implies that most of the Chinese have been socialized in such a manner that they do not easily let their primitive passions and impulses be completely expressed, at least not publicly (Kindle, 1982). Given Chinese people's general tendency to control impulses and refrain from expressive spontaneity, it is probable that they would not be as emotionally responsive to in-store environmental cues as their Western counterparts.

Despite the plausibility of this inference, as far as leisure consumption is concerned, the impact of Chinese people's low impulsivity should not be exaggerated. Although the Chinese are, in general, found to be good at controlling their impulses, their spontaneity in expressing their emotions seems to be sphere-specific or to vary across situations. As reported in previous research, the Chinese tend to express their emotions rather spontaneously when the subject matter in question involves nature, the physical environment, or food (Yang, 1993). Logically, their spontaneity in expressing their emotions toward an environment should be greater if the reason for their presence in that environment is mainly to get personal pleasures. Taken together, this sphere theory provides support to the applicability of the Environment-Emotion-Behavior framework among Chinese consumers.

THE PROPOSED MODEL AND HYPOTHESES

This paper builds on Mehrabian and Russell's (1974) framework (see Figure 1). A model trying to explain the major antecedents and consequences of Chinese consumer's emotional responses in a game center setting is depicted in Figure 2. The model specifically advocates that consumer's perceived physical environment of a game center (game center physical environment or GCPEnv) will directly affect their emotional states or level of excitement (Excite). The affected emotional states (Excite), in turn, will have a significant bearing on their behavioral responses in terms of instant resource expenditure (RExp) in the center and repatronage intention (RInt) in the future. Similar studies have been attempted by researchers before but the evidence is quite limited in general and very rare in a Chinese cultural context. Therefore, three of the hypotheses tested by Wakefield and Blodgett (1996, 1999) are included here for the purposes of confirmatory testing.

H1:   A positively perceived environment of a game center would have a positive influence on Chinese consumers' level of excitement.

H2:   Chinese consumers' increased level of excitement experienced in a game center will have a positive influence on their resource expenditure there.

H3:   Chinese consumers' increased level of excitement experienced in a game center will have a positive influence on their repatronage intention.

In addition to the foregoing three hypotheses, two additional hypotheses have been developed and read as follows:

H4: A positively perceived environment of a game center would have a positive influence on Chinese consumers' repatronage intention.

H5: Chinese consumers' increased resource expenditure in a game center will have a positive influence on their repatronage intention.

The development of the fourth hypothesis aims to distinguish between the affective and cognitive influences of the perceived physical environment on shoppers' future behavioral responses. While it was hypothesized earlier that the perceived physical environment would have an indirect positive effect on repatronage intention via the mediating variable, excitement (shopping emotions), hypothesis four further postulates a direct positive influence of the environment on repatronage intention. As a general belief, the indirect effect should be more concerned with shoppers' immediate affective responses toward various environmental cues of a service outlet (Wakefield and Blodgett, 1999). As such, their willingness to repatronize the outlet via this indirect route should be more to do with their emotional attachment to the outlet than their elaborate cognitive evaluation of its entire service package.

On the other hand, it is thought that a shopper's perception of the physical environment of a service outlet should have a direct influence on his repatronage intention as well. The direct influence should be more concerned with his cognitive evaluation of the environmental stimuli he has received through his perceptual process. As proposed by perceptual theories, consumers often form associations and draw inferences between stimuli. Through their perceptual process, they often develop beliefs about offerings of a store based upon their own experiences with the stimuli to which they are exposed (Hanna and

FIGURE 2. The Proposed Model and Hypotheses

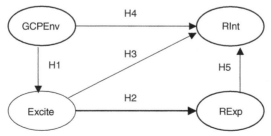

Notes:
GCPEnv - perceived physical environment of the game center
Excite - excitement
RInt - repatronage intention
RExp - resource expenditure

Wozniak, 2000). Conceivably, such stimuli would also include various environmental cues of the store. The hypothesized direct influence of the perceived physical environment on repatronage intention is thus aimed to capture the effect of the foregoing cognitive evaluation.

The formulation of the fifth hypothesis follows the rationale put forward by Wakefield and Baker (1998) in studying American shopper's emotional responses at the mall level. These two researchers maintain that if shoppers enjoy spending more of their resources (e.g., time and money) in the retail setting due to favorable perception of the physical environment, they should also be more ready to repatronize and spend resources in the same setting in the future. In other words, what these two researchers have put forward is based on the premise that present behavioral responses should serve as a reasonable predictor of future ones.

METHODOLOGY

Measurement Instruments

To test the validity of the proposed model and all the hypothesized relationships therein, a survey approach was employed. While English was initially used to develop the survey questionnaire, it was subsequently translated into Chinese to facilitate Chinese respondent's understanding. The "linguistic equivalence" of the English and Chinese versions was ensured by employing Bhalla and Lin's (1987) suggested back translation techniques. The measurement instruments for all the relevant constructs were developed based on previous relevant literature (e.g., Babin and Darden, 1995; Oliver and Swan, 1989; Wakefield and Baker, 1998). To suit the local environment and the purpose of the present study, the questionnaire was further polished and modified according to input from two focus group's discussions. The adopted instruments are detailed in Appendix I for reference. Briefly, the items for measuring the three perceived physical environmental factors (ambience, design, and layout), excitement and repatronage intention, were developed according to Wakefield and Baker's (1998) approach. Furthermore, following the suggestion for future research made by these two researchers, the exact length of time and amount of money spent in the outlet, rather than intervally-coded items, were employed to measure the construct of resource expenditure in this study.

Relating specifically to the operationalization of the construct of perceived physical environment, one methodological issue warrants further mention here. In Wakefield and Baker's (1998) empirical study using structural equation modeling, such a construct was first conceptualized as a second-order factor accounting for the influence of three first-order factors, ambience, design and layout. Based on this proposed factor structure, these two researchers then developed a number of items to measure each of the three first-order factors. However, their empirical results did indicate inter-correlations between ambience, layout, and design, as well as between items within each of these three factors. Given that "individuals are apt to perceive the physical environment in a holistic manner," the two researchers considered that these findings were "not unexpected" (Wakefield and Baker, 1998, p. 527). To address the inter-correlation issue, they therefore modified the factor structure of perceived physical environment by treating it as a first-order factor and having ambience, design and layout serve as its three indicators. As can be seen later, the same modification was applied in this study, and this will be described in detail in the subsequent "results" section.

The Sample

The survey was conducted in four large game shops located in the major shopping area of the city of Guangzhou, China. Fifty patrons from each of the four game centers (GCs) were interviewed, resulting in a total sample size of 200. Trained local fieldworkers were hired to administer the fieldwork by asking every fifth patron exiting the center to complete the survey. Overall, 57 percent of the respondents were male, 31 percent of them were aged between eighteen and twenty-five, and 28 percent were between twenty-six and thirty. Regarding their occupation, 19%, 15%, 22% and 13% of the respondents were professionals, managers, white-collar workers and students respectively. Their median monthly personal income was between US $190 and US $220, and three-quarters of them had finished high school. Except for a higher income level, the demographic profile of the respondents was found to be compatible with that of the entire Guangzhou population (at χ^2 significance of $p < 0.05$) (cf. *China Statistical Yearbook,* 1999). The exception highlights the entertaining nature of the service under investigation. As the service is far from a daily necessity, it is not unreasonable for higher earning individuals to patronize it more frequently.

Results

To assess the reliability and validity of the proposed model, Gerbing and Anderson's (1988) recommended two-step procedure was referred to. According to this procedure, the validity of the relevant constructs was first examined before validating the full structural model. To accomplish the first task, reliability test, exploratory factor analysis and confirmatory factor analysis were employed accordingly, and the relevant detail is described below.

Specifically, the Cronbach Alpha reliability test was first performed on all the constructs under investigation (ambient factor, design factor, layout factor, excitement, repatronage intention, and resource expenditure) to see whether the proposed measurement items (cf. Appendix I) constituted reliable measures of the constructs they were designed to represent. Except for the construct of repatronage intention, all the constructs rendered acceptable Cronbach Alpha coefficients larger than 0.70 (cf. Nunnually, 1978). The Cronbach Alpha coefficient of repatronage intention was only equal to 0.54. A closer examination of the respective reliability contribution of the three constituent measurement items (Rint1 to Rint3) of this constructs indicated that the removal of RInt3 (cf. Appendix I) would raise the Cronbach Alpha coefficient to 0.71. Based on this, Rint3 was thus removed from the subsequent analysis.

To further assess the reliability, six different exploratory factor analyses were then performed on the six sets of measurement items: (1) A1 to A4; (2) D1 to D4; (3) L1 to L4; (3) Excite1 to Excite5; (4) Rint1 to Rint2; and (5) RExp1 to Rexp2. These six sets were aimed at measuring the constructs of ambient factor, design factor, layout factor, excitement, repatronage intention, and resource expenditure respectively (cf. Appendix I). By setting the cut-off eigenvalue value at 1.0 and employing varimax rotation to facilitate interpretation, the factor analyses showed that all the measurement items were loaded on the constructs they were proposed to represent. This finding provides further evidence of the reliability of the measures.

In view of the above findings, confirmatory factor analysis (CFA) was further performed to assess the fitness of the proposed measurement model (cf. Hair et al., 1995). In order words, the analysis was aimed at examining whether the proposed measurement items represented valid indicators of the constructs under investigation. Such examination is regarded as an important first step to ensure the validity of the constructs before running the full structural equation analysis (Byrne, 1994; Hair et al., 1995).

The CFA was conducted by using the structural equation modeling software, EQS 5.7b (cf. Bentler, 1995; Bentler and Wu, 1995). Echoing Wakefield and Baker's (1998) findings, the CFA based on the originally proposed factor structure also suggested inter-correlations between the ambience, layout, and design, and inter-item correlations within each of these factors. As mentioned earlier, this observation was considered not uncommon as individuals tend to perceive the physical environment in a holistic manner (Bitner, 1992; Wakefield and Baker, 1998). This is especially so for those who are culturally inclined to view things holistically, such as the Chinese (Hwang, 1982; Yang, 1993).

To cope with the inter-correlation issue, the aforementioned modification procedure of Wakefield and Baker (1998, pp. 526-27) was adopted here. Specifically, the construct of perceived physical environment (referred to as "game center physical environment" or GCPEnv hereafter) was changed from a second-order factor to a first-order one. In addition, ambience, design and layout were treated as three indicators of the perceived physical environment.

The creation of these three new indicators (i.e., ambience, design, and layout) was done by summing up the scores of their constituent items. To illustrate, scores on items A1 to A4 depicted in Appendix I were summed up to represent the indicator of ambience. Similarly, scores on items D1 to D4, and those on items L1 to L4 were summed up to represent the design and layout indicators respectively.

It should be noted that the aforementioned modification procedure only involved collapsing the *measurement items* of ambience, design and layout, it did not involve collapsing themselves into any single dimension. Instead, ambience, design and layout were treated as three *separate* indicators to define the construct (or first-order factor) of perceived physical environment. In other words, the modified factor structure is still able to show the contribution each of these three indicators made to define the perceived physical environment. As reflected by the CFA factor loadings shown in the second column of Table 1, such contribution of ambience, design and layout was equal to 0.70, 0.84 and 0.70 respectively.

Table 1 summarizes the CFA results after the aforementioned modifications were made to the CFA or measurement model. To assess the overall fitness of the measurement model, a number of commonly used fit indexes such as the Goodness-of-Fit Index (GFI), Comparative Fit Index (CFI) and Root Mean Square Error of Approximation (RMSEA) were referred to. To summarize, the computed GFI (0.933) and CFI (0.910) were both above the recommended threshold of 0.90 (Byrne, 1994; Hair et al., 1995). In addition, the RMSEA was equal to 0.069 and within the acceptable limit of 0.1 (Browne and Cudeck, 1993). Relating specifically to the assessment of convergent and discriminant validity, the CFA results also showed that all indicators were loaded on the hypothesized constructs, and the pairwise comparisons of all the relevant constructs showed that their correlations were significantly different from 1.0 (cf. Fornell and Larcker, 1981; Kim and Frazier, 1997). Taken together, the CFA results showed an adequate fit of the measurement model.

Analysis of the Full Structural Model

Based on the satisfactory results derived from the CFA, the full structural analysis was performed according to the two-stage approach suggested by Gerbing and Anderson (1988). The full structural analysis was aimed at testing the overall fitness of the proposed model as well as the hypothesized relationships among the constructs under investigtation (c.f. Figure 2). The overall fitness was assessed by referring to such commonly employed fit indexes as GFI, CFI and RMSEA. As noted from Figure 3, the GFI and CFI were found to be 0.932 and 0.907 respectively, and exceeded the acceptable threshold of 0.90 (cf. Byrne, 1994; Hair et al., 1995). In addition, the RMSEA was equal to 0.70

TABLE 1. Summarized CFA results of the Measurement Model (N = 200)

Construct Item/Indicator	GCPEnv	Excite	RInt	RExp
Ambience (A1-A4)	0.70[a]			
Design (D1-D4)	0.84*			
Layout (L1-L4)	0.70*			
Excite1		0.75[a]		
Excite2		0.87*		
Excite3		0.32*		
Excite4		0.55*		
Excite5		0.31*		
RInt1			0.57[a]	
RInt2			0.96*	
RExp1				0.53[a]
RExp2				0.77*

$\chi^2_{\text{null model}} = 571.035$ (df = 66); $\chi^2_{\text{proposed model}} = 93.306$ (df = 48, $p < 0.001$)[#];
GFI = 0.933; CFI = 0.910; RMSEA = 0.069

Notes:
GCPEnv, Excite, RInt and RExp refer to perceived physical environment of the game center, excitement, repatronage intention and resource expenditure respectively. For a more detailed description of the indicators, please refer to Appendix I.
[a]   Initially fixed at 1 for estimation purpose.
*   Significantly at $p < 0.05$.
#   Although the χ^2 sig. was smaller than the recommended threshold of 0.05, it has long been commented that χ^2 statistic is sensitive to sample size and rejection of a model solely based on it is inappropriate (Bagozzi and Yi, 1988; Marsh et al., 1988). Indeed, other fit indexes reported above all show an acceptable fit of the proposed measurement model.

and within the acceptable limit of 0.1 (cf. Browne and Cudeck, 1993). These values all suggest an acceptable fit of the proposed model (i.e., the full structural model) depicted in Figure 2.

In addition to the findings concerning the overall fitness of the full structural model, Figure 3 also shows the standardized path estimates of the model. These estimates can help to test the five hypotheses formulated earlier. To summarize, except for the path estimates for Excitement → Repatronage Intention (H3), and Resource Expenditure → Repatronage Intention (H5), all the other three estimates were significant at $p < 0.05$. Deviating from what has been hypothesized, the insignificant path estimate of Excitement → Repatronage Intention was also reported to be negative rather than positive.

The three significant estimates related to the path of Perceived Physical Environment → Excitement (H1), Excitement → Resource Expenditure (H2),

FIGURE 3. Summarized Results of the Structural Analysis

Summarized Fit Indexes:

$\chi^2_{\text{null model}} = 571.035$, df = 66

$\chi^2_{\text{proposed model}} = 96.013$, df = 49, p < 0.001[#]

GFI = 0.932; CFI = 0.907; RMSEA = 0.070

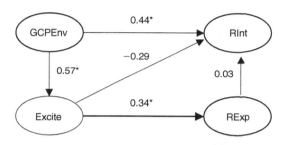

Notes:

GCPEnv	- perceived physical environment of the game center
Excite	- excitement
RInt	- repatronage intention
RExp	- resource expenditure

Path figures represent the estimated standardized path coefficients.

* Significantly at p < 0.05.

[#] Although the χ^2 sig. was smaller than the recommended threshold of 0.05, it has long been commented that χ^2 statistic is sensitive to sample size and rejection of a model solely based on it is inappropriate (Bagozzi and Yi, 1988; Marsh et al., 1988). Indeed, other fit indexes reported above all show an acceptable fit of the proposed full structural model.

and Perceived Physical Environment → Repatronage Intention (H4). In addition, the sign (+ or −) of these three significant estimates were all consistent with the hypotheses put forward earlier. Taken together, the above results provide support to hypotheses one, two, and four. In other words, the results of the full structural analysis confirm the belief that the perceived physical environment of the game center exerts a direct and positive influence on consumer's emotional state (i.e., excitement) as well as on their repatronage intention. They also indicate that if such an environment really makes customers feel excited, their excitement will, in turn, induce them to spend more resources (resource expenditure) in the center.

DISCUSSION

Not all of the hypothesized paths in the model are supported by the empirical findings in this study. A summary of the results is given below.

Hypothesis		Result
H1	A positively perceived environment of a game center will have a positive influence on Chinese consumers' level of excitement.	supported
H2	Chinese consumers' increased level of excitement experienced in a game center will have a positive influence on their resource expenditure there.	supported
H3	Chinese consumers' increased level of excitement experienced in a game center will have a positive influence on their repatronage intention.	rejected
H4	A positively perceived environment of a game center will have a positive influence on Chinese consumers' repatronage intention.	supported
H5	Chinese consumers' increased resource expenditure in a game center will have a positive influence on their repatronage intention.	rejected

This study illustrates that the service environment (ambience, design, and layout) has an effect on both consumer's affective and cognitive responses. On the affective side, environmental cues exert a significant influence on consumer's excitement level, in that a positively perceived physical environment is associated with their pleasant feelings. The increased level of excitement, in turn, is found to affect positively the amount of resources (time and money) they spend in the game center. Concerning the cognitive side, this study provides some support to the inference that the perceived physical environment does have a direct impact on consumer's repatronage intention via their perceptual process of in-store environmental stimuli. However, no relationship has been found between excitement level and repatronage intention, or between resource expenditure and repatronage intention. In other words, instant environment-provoked emotional arousal affects the immediate behavior (resource expenditure) of the consumer only, and it has no influence on his future intended behavior (repatronage).

The ability of environments to affect shopper emotions, and of these emotions to affect shopping behavior has been demonstrated in several studies. The environments of these studies are concerned with various kinds of retail outlets such as department stores, discount stores, specialty stores, and banks (Babin and Darden, 1995; Dawson et al., 1990; Foxall and Greenley, 1999). Given that consumers nowadays view the retail outlet not only as a place for shopping, but also for entertainment (Bloch et al., 1994), the results of these previous studies may be equally applicable to other leisure service settings such as game centers. Indeed, when the results of the present study are compared with some earlier servicescape studies concerning such leisure environments as football stadiums, baseball fields, and casinos (cf. Bitner, 1992;

Wakefield and Blodgett, 1996), it is found that they, to a large extent, echo each other. The major difference concerns the repatronage intention. While previous studies, in general, confirm the positive relationship between "desire to stay"/"shopping time"/"shopping expenditure" and "repatronage intention," and between "excitement"/"emotion" and "repatronage intention," the findings of the present study provide no support of the same.

While the lack of a significant relationship between resource expenditure and repatronage intention is difficult to reconcile and thus calls for future research attention, the insignificant influence of excitement on repatronage intention may suggest that such intention is influenced by, in addition to the service environment (ambience, design, and layout), other factors not included in the model. Potential contributors to repatronage include other game center characteristics, such as size, geographic location, game mix, price, and service staff performance; as well as consumer characteristics, such as self-regulation, variety-seeking tendency, and involvement with games. These factors may well influence excitement, but probably to a different extent. The discrepancy between the present study results and those from previous studies in the West may suggest that the influences of these missing factors on repatronage intention are stronger in a Chinese cultural context. In any event, this foregoing issue warrants further exploration in future studies.

As a plausible explanation, cultural differences may account for the aforementioned insignificant relationship between excitement and repatronage intention. In the consumer research literature, cultural values have long been recognized as a powerful force in shaping consumer motivations, lifestyles, and product choices (Lowe and Corkindale, 1998). Although it can be argued that the spread of Western consumption patterns and popular culture might have influenced Asian values, the central or core values of these societies have yet to be westernized (Huntington, 1996). The religious and cultural traditions of the East and West are deeply ingrained in people's attitudes (Kugler, 1998). Many studies have illustrated the differences between Western and Asian service consumer's perceptions of service quality. For example, Japanese and Western students gave differential ratings to many behaviors of restaurant employees (Winsted, 1997). Another example is found in a study by Mattila (1999) in which Asian leisure travelers gave significantly lower ratings to the service encounter and overall service quality compared to their Western counterparts.

It is generally believed that Chinese people put a strong emphasis on purchase value and a low emphasis on the product's/service's aesthetic dimensions (Tse, 1996). If they have to spend, they are motivated to obtain the same performance at a lower price, thus yielding a higher purchase value. A higher return for their money would be strongly preferred. The price factor will therefore be a major issue when considering a re-purchase.

Broadly speaking, service styles in Asia are more people-oriented than in the West, where the efficiency of the service delivery is highly valued (Riddle, 1992). In the service culture of Asia, even consumers of low-cost services expect a relatively high level of service (Schmitt and Pan, 1994). Malhotra et al. (1994) also suggest that reliability of services can be better established with a relative emphasis on personnel in developing countries like China, and a relative emphasis on technology in developed countries like the US. The fact that Chinese consumers place a primary emphasis on the quality of interpersonal relationships and the kind of service they receive in the game center may constitute a key factor in their service-encounter evaluation.

Another variable that might explain the differences relates not so much to culture but more to the development stage of the game center business in different economies. Consumers are apt to invest considerable search effort in comparison shopping at some point before settling into a patronage routine (Urbany et al., 1996). In Guangzhou, where this study was conducted, game centers are still in the growth stage. As such, consumers there are likely to continue shopping around among various game centers for some time to come before they assign their loyalty to a particular center.

CONCLUSIONS

The findings provide support for the central premise of this paper, that physical environment is an important determinant of consumer responses when the service is consumed primarily for hedonic purposes in a leisure-oriented service setting. It applies in Western as well as in Chinese cultures, despite the fact that many researchers have suggested that Chinese consumers may adopt unique consumption characteristics (Cheng, 1994; Lee and Tse, 1994). Service providers therefore should make every effort to ensure that the ambience, design, and layout match, as closely as possible, the tastes and preferences of their customers. In addition to paying close attention to all aspects of the service environment during the design stages, executives of service operations should continually track the possible changes of their customer's perceptions and repatronage intention to ensure corporate success.

To conclude, the environment in which a service is consumed–whether or not it is for hedonic experiences–is an area to which services marketers need to pay greater attention. The physical environment may assume a variety of strategic roles in services marketing and management. The dimensions of the service surroundings act as a package, similar to a product offering, by conveying a total image and suggesting the potential usage and relative quality of the service.

REFERENCES

Apple Daily (2000). Cars Are No Longer Luxurious Items for the Mainland Chinese, October 26, A25.

Babin, Barry J.; Darden, William R. and Griffin, M. (1994). Work and/or Fun: Measuring Hedonic and Utilitarian Shopping Value, *Journal of Consumer Research*, 20, 644-656.

Babin, Barry J. and Darden, William R. (1995). Consumer Self-regulation in a Retail Environment, *Journal of Retailing*, 71 (1), 47-70.

Bentler, P. M. (1995). *EQS–Structural Equations Program Manual*, California, Multivariate Software Inc.

Bentler, P. M. and Wu, E. J. C. (1995). *EQS for Windows: User's Guide*, California, Multivariate Software, Inc.

Bhalla, G. and Lin, L. (1987). Cross-cultural Marketing Research: A Discussion of Equivalence Issues and Measurement Strategies, *Psychology and Marketing*, 4, 275-285.

Bitner, M. J. (1992). Servicescapes: The Impact of Physical Surroundings on Customers and Employees, *Journal of Marketing*, 56 (2), 57-72.

Bloch, Peter H., Ridgway, Nancy M. and Dawson, Scott A. (1994). The Shopping Mall as Consumer Habitat, *Journal of Retailing*, 70 (1), 23-42.

Browne, M. W. and Cudeck, R. (1993). Alternative Ways of Assessing Model Fit. In *Testing Structural Equation Models* (pp. 136-162), K. Bollen and J. S. Long (eds.), Thousand Oaks, CA, Sage Publications.

Byrne, B. M. (1994). *Structural Equation Modeling with EQS and EQS/Windows*, London, Sage Publications.

Cheng, C. K. (1946). Characteristic Traits of the Chinese People, *Social Forces*, 25, 146-155.

Cheng, H (1994). Reflections of Cultural Values: A Content Analysis of Chinese Magazine Advertisements from 1982 to 1992, *International Journal of Advertising*, 13, 167-183.

China Statistical Yearbook (1999), Beijing, China Statistics Press.

Cui, Geng (1997). The Different Faces of the Chinese Consumer, *China Business Review*, 24 (4), July/August, 34-39.

Darden, William R. and Babin, Barry J. (1994). Exploring the Concept of Affective Quality: Expanding the Concept of Retail Personality, *Journal of Business Research*, 29 (February), 101-109.

Dawson, Scott, Bloch, Peter H. and Ridgway, Nancy M. (1990). Shopping Motives, Emotional States, and Retail Outcomes, *Journal of Retailing*, 66 (Winter), 408-427.

Donovan, R. J. and Rossiter, J (1982). Store Atmosphere: An Environmental Psychology Approach, *Journal of Retailing*, 58 (Spring), 34-57.

Donovan, R. J., Rossiter, J. R., Marcoolyn, G. and Nesdale, A. (1994). Store Atmosphere and Purchasing Behavior, *Journal of Retailing*, 70 (3), 283-294.

Fornell, C. and Larcker, D. F. (1981). Evaluating Structural Equation Models with Unobservable Variables and Measurement Error, *Journal of Marketing Research*, 18, 39-50.

Foxall, Gordon R. and Greenley, Gorden E. (1999). Consumer's Emotional Responses to Service Environments, *Journal of Business Research*, 46, 149-158.

Gardner, M.P. (1985). Mood States and Consumer Behavior: A Critical Review, *Journal of Consumer Research*, 12 (December), 281-300.

Gerbing, D. W. and Anderson, J. C. (1988). An Updated Paradigm for Scale Development Incorporating Unidimensionality and Its Assessment, *Journal of Marketing Research*, 25 (May), 186-192.

Hair, Joseph F., Anderson, Rolph E., Tatham, Ronald L. and Black, William C. (1995). *Multivariate Data Analysis with Readings*, New Jersey, Prentice Hall.

Hanna, Nessim and Wozniak, Richard (2000). *Consumer Behavior: An Applied Approach*, New Jersey, Prentice-Hall.

Herrington, J. D. and Capella, L. M. (1996). Effects of Music in Service Environments: A Field Study, *Journal of Services Marketing*, 10 (2), 26-41.

Hsu, F. L. K. (1949). Suppression Versus Repression: A Limited Psychological Interpretation of Four Cultures, *Psychiatry*, 12, 223-242.

Huntington, S. (1996). *The Clash of Civilizations and the Remaking of World Order*, New York, Simon and Schuster.

Hwang, C. H. (1982). Studies in Chinese Personality: A Critical Review, *Bulletin of Education Psychology*, 15, 227-240.

Kim, K. and Frazier, G. L. (1997). Measurement of Distributor Commitment in Industrial Channels of Distribution, *Journal of Business Research*, 40, 139-154.

Kindle, I. (1982). A Partial Theory of Chinese Consumer Behavior: Marketing Strategy Implications, *Hong Kong Journal of Business Management*, 1, 97-109.

Kluckhohn, F. R. and Strodtbeck, F. L. (1961). *Variations in Value Orientations*, Illinois, Row, Paterson and Company.

Kugler, R. (1998). Tigers Don't Change their Stripes: East Asian Consumer Trends and the Economic Downturn, *Journal of Brand Management*, 5, 94-9.

Lee, W. and Tse, D.K. (1994). Becoming Canadian: Understanding How Hong Kong Immigrants Change their Consumption, *Pacific Affairs*, 67 (1), 70-96.

Li, C. (1997). *China: The Consumer Revolution*, New York, Deloitte and Touche Consulting Group.

Lowe, Anthony Chun-Tung and Corkindale, David R. (1998). Differences in Cultural Values and their Effects on Marketing Stimuli, *European Journal of Marketing*, 32 (9/10), 479-506.

Malhotra, Naresh K.; Ulgado, Francis M.; Agarwal, James and Baalbaki, Imad B. (1994). International Services Marketing: A Comparative Evaluation of the Dimensions of Service Quality between Developed and Developing Countries, *International Marketing Review*, 11 (2), 5-15.

Mattila, Anna S. (1999). The Role of Culture and Purchase Motivation in Service Encounter Evaluation, *Journal of Services Marketing*, 13 (4/5), 376-389.

McCloud, John (1999). US Shopping Centers Thrive as Hubs of Entertainment, *National Real Estate Investor*, 41 (6) May, 42-55.

Mehrabian, A. and Russell, J. A. (1974). *An Approach to Environmental Psychology*, Cambridge, MA, MIT Press.

Miller, D. (1988). Relating Porter's Business Strategies to Environment and Structure: Analysis and Performance Implications, *Academy of Management Journal*, 31, 280-308.

Nunnally, J. C. (1978). *Psychometric Theory*, New York, McGraw-Hill.

Oliver, R. L. and Swan, J. E. (1989). Consumer Perceptions of Interpersonal Equity and Satisfaction in Transactions: A Field Survey Approach, *Journal of Marketing*, 53 (April), 21-35.

Riddle, D. (1992). Leveraging Cultural Factors in International Service Delivery, *Advances in Services Marketing and Management*, 1, 297-322.

Ridgway, Nancy M.; Bloch, Peter H. and Nelson, James E. (1994). A Neglected P: The Importance of Place in Consumer Response, working paper, University of Colorado, Boulder, CO.

Russell, James A. and Pratt, G. (1980). A Description of the Affective Quality Attributed to Environments, *Journal of Personality and Social Psychology*, 38, 311-322.

Russell, James A. and Yik, Michelle S. M. (1996). Emotion among the Chinese. In Michael Harris, Bond (Ed.) *The Handbook of Chinese Psychology* (pp. 166-188), Hong Kong, Oxford University Press.

Schmitt, B. and Pan, Y.(1994). Managing Corporate and Brand Identities in the Asia-Pacific Region, *California Management Review*, 36 (4), 32-48.

Tai, Susan H.C. Susan and Fung, Agnes M.C. (1997). Application of Environmental Psychology Model to In-Store Buying Behavior, *International Review of Retail, Distribution and Consumer Research*, 7 (4) October, 311-337.

Tse, David K. (1996). Understanding Chinese People as Consumers: Past Findings and Future Propositions. In *The Handbook of Chinese Psychology* (pp. 352-363), Michael Harris, Bond (Ed.), Hong Kong, Oxford University Press.

Tseng, W. S. (1973). The Concept of Personality in Confucian Thought. *Psychiatry*, 36, 191-202.

Urbany, Joel E.; Dickson, Peter B. and Kalapurakal, Rosemary (1996). Price Search in the Retail Grocery Market, *Journal of Marketing*, 60 (April), 91-104.

Wakefield, Kirl L. and Baker, J. (1998). Excitement at the Mall: Determinants and Effects on Shopping Response, *Journal of Retailing*, 74 (4), 515-539.

Wakefield, Kirk L. and Blodgett, Jeffrey G. (1994). The Importance of Servicescapes in Leisure Service Settings, *Journal of Services Marketing*, 8 (3), 66-76.

Wakefield, Kirk L. and Blodgett, Jeffrey G. (1996). The Effect of the Servicescape on Customer's Behavioral Intentions in Leisure Service Setting, *Journal of Services Marketing*, 10 (6), 45-61.

Wakefield, Kirk L. and Blodgett, Jeffrey G. (1999). Customer Response to Intangible and Tangible Service Factors, *Psychology and Marketing*, 16 (1), 51-68.

Wakefield, Kirk L. and Bush, Victoria D. (1998). Promoting Leisure Services: Economic and Emotional Aspects of Consumer Response, *Journal of Services Marketing*, 12 (3), 209-222.

Winsted, K. (1997). The Service Experience in Two Cultures: A Behavioral Perspective, *Journal of Retailing*, 73, 337-60.

Wirtz, Jochen and Bateson, John E. G. (1999). Consumer Satisfaction with Services: Integrating the Environment Perspective in Services Marketing into the Traditional Disconfirmation Paradigm, *Journal of Business Research*, 44, 55-66.

Yang, K. S. (1993). Chinese Personality and its Change. In: *The Psychology of the Chinese People* (pp. 106-160), Michael Harris, Bond (ed.), Hong Kong, Oxford University Press.

Yau, Oliver H. M. (1994). *Consumer Behavior in China: Customer Satisfaction and Cultural Values*, London, Routledge.

APPENDIX I. Description of the Measurement Instruments

Game Center Physical Environment (GCPEnv):

1. Ambient factor (Ambience)*
A1 -   The GC plays music that I like.
A2 -   The GC music is played at an appropriate volume.
A3 -   The GC lighting is appropriate.
A4 -   The GC temperature is comfortable.

2. Design factor*
D1 -   The GC's architecture gives it an attractive character.
D2 -   The GC is decorated in an attractive fashion.
D3 -   The interior wall and floor color schemes of the GC are attractive.
D4 -   The overall design of the GC is interesting.

3. Layout factor*
L1 -   The layout of the GC makes it easy to find the games I want.
L2 -   The layout of the GC makes it easy to find those racing games.
L3 -   The layout of the GC makes it easy to get to the restrooms.
L4 -   Overall, the layout of the GC makes it easy to get around.

Excitement (Excite)*
This GC is:
Excite1 -   unexciting/exciting
Excite2 -   dull/interesting
Excite3 -   boring/stimulating
Excite4 -   unappealing/appealing
Excite5 -   monotonous/sensational

Repatronage Intention (RInt)*
In the future, my patronage of this GC will be:
RInt1 -   not at all/very frequent
RInt2 -   not probable/very probable
RInt3 -   unlikely/likely#

Resource Expenditure (RExp)**

RExp1 -   The number of minutes I spent in this GC is: _____ (minutes).
RExp2 -   The amount of money I spent in this GC is: _____ (Renminbi).

Notes:
GC refers to game center.
A1 to A4, D1 to D4 and L1 to L4 were coded on 5-point disagree-agree scales.
Excite1 to Excite5 and RInt1 to RInt2 were coded on 7-point semantic differential scales
*   Items adopted from Wakefield and Baker (1998).
**   RExp1 and RExp2 were normalized to common metrics before analysis.
#   Removed from the final analysis based on results from the reliability test and CFA.

Consumer Processing
of International Advertising:
The Roles of Country of Origin
and Consumer Ethnocentrism

Byeong-Joon Moon
Subhash C. Jain

SUMMARY. This research examines the impacts of consumer's two crossnational individual difference variables–country-of-origin perception and consumer ethnocentrism–on their responses and attitudes toward foreign advertisements. Empirical analysis of the hypothetical model through structural equation modeling yields supportive results: negative effects of consumer's ethnocentrism on their responses to the creative presentation of international advertising, and positive effects of consumer's country-of-origin perceptions on their responses to the buying proposal of international advertising. This study may contribute to our understanding of cross-national individual difference variables that precede and determine consumers' attitudes toward international advertising. It also has practical implications for the standardization versus localization debate in international advertising strategy. *[Article copies available for a fee from The Haworth Document Delivery Service: 1-800-342-9678. E-mail address: <getinfo@haworthpressinc.com> Website: <http://www.HaworthPress. com> © 2001 by The Haworth Press, Inc. All rights reserved.]*

Byeong-Joon Moon is affiliated with the School of International Management, KyungHee University, Yongin-shi Kyunggi-do 449-701, South Korea (E-mail: bmoon@ khu.ac.kr). Subhash C. Jain is affiiated with the Department of Marketing, University of Connecticut, 368 Fairfield Road, U-41MK, Storrs, CT 06269-2041.

[Haworth co-indexing entry note]: "Consumer Processing of International Advertising: The Roles of Country of Origin and Consumer Ethnocentrism." Moon, Byeong-Joon, and Subhash C. Jain. Co-published simultaneously in *Journal of International Consumer Marketing* (International Business Press, an imprint of The Haworth Press, Inc.) Vol. 14, No. 1, 2001, pp. 89-109; and: *Asian Dimensions of Services Marketing* (ed: Esther P. Y. Tang, Ricky Y. K. Chan, and Susan H. C. Tai) International Business Press, an imprint of The Haworth Press, Inc., 2001, pp. 89-109. Single or multiple copies of this article are available for a fee from The Haworth Document Delivery Service [1-800-342-9678, 9:00 a.m. - 5:00 p.m. (EST). E-mail address: getinfo@haworthpressinc.com].

89

KEYWORDS. Consumer response, international advertising strategy, buying proposal, creative presentation, country-of-origin perception, consumer ethnocentrism

The globalization of markets and expansion of firms operating internationally has led to the increase of international advertising. Consumers in global markets are exposed to a wider range of foreign products and advertising than ever before. As a result, marketers have shown a burgeoning interest in understanding the factors related to consumers' responses to international advertising and their decision making in regard to foreign products. This research focuses on consumers' psychological processing of advertising that promotes a foreign product (brand) in that country's own cultural context. We refer to this type of advertising as "foreign advertising." Foreign advertising is not very common in the U.S. Since the size of the U.S. economy is very large, almost all advertising for foreign country-of-origin products is localized to fit American culture. However foreign advertising is not uncommon in other countries. For example, advertisements that promote American brands in an American cultural context are pervasive in countries such as Japan and South Korea, even though the cultural differences between those countries and the U.S. are extreme. The objective of this research is to understand how consumer's cross-national individual difference variables–country-of-origin perceptions and consumer ethnocentrism–affect their responses and attitudes toward foreign advertisements.

Although research on the subject of consumer processing of international advertising is slim, literature on consumer behavior in the United States and cross-national comparative studies of advertising provide useful insights into this area. Cross-national individual difference variables that have been studied extensively in foreign product consumption are those related to country-of-origin and consumer ethnocentrism. Research on country-of-origin effects (e.g., Hong and Wyer 1989) indicates that consumers develop stereotypical images of products made in particular countries, which subsequently affect their purchase decisions. Studies on consumer ethnocentrism (e.g., Shimp and Sharma 1987) show that consumer's patriotic prejudices against imports result in more favorable evaluations of domestic products vis-à-vis imported products. Cross-national comparative studies on consumer response to advertising (e.g., Hornik 1980) and literature on international marketing strategy (e.g., Jain 1989) suggest that cultural and psychological differences between countries be considered when developing international advertising strategy. However, there has been little research on consumer processing of international advertising; specifically, the roles of these cross-national individual difference variables in consumer processing of foreign advertisements have been neglected. This research examines two critical elements, buying proposal and creative presentation (Killough 1978), in the transfer of advertising across nations to understand why some concepts (e.g., localization strategy) work while others (e.g., standardization strategy) do not and to improve the chances for getting better results.

THEORETICAL FRAMEWORK

Our model for understanding consumer processing of foreign advertising is displayed in Figure 1. Consumer's two cross-national individual difference variables–country-of-origin perceptions and consumer ethnocentrism–affect their attitudes toward a foreign advertisement. These effects are mediated through responses to creative presentation and buying proposal of a foreign advertisement.

Dual Elements of International Advertising

Killough (1978) argued that advertising propositions for international transfer consist of two elements which must be considered separately because the

FIGURE 1. Hypothetical Structural Equation Model

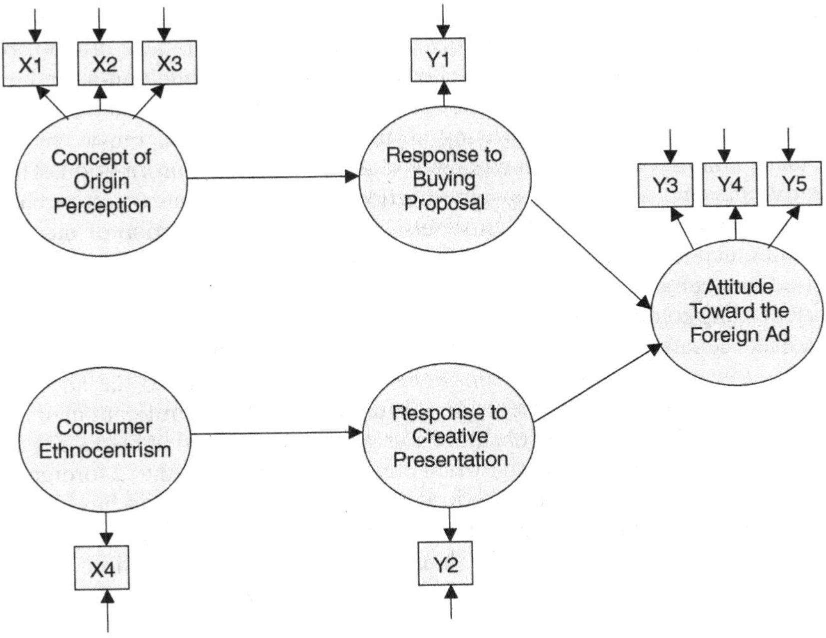

reaction to them is different in different countries. He differentiated between "buying proposal," that states the basic offer, and "creative presentation," that packages the buying proposal. However, Killough's demarcation of the two elements of international advertising propositions is fuzzy. Clearer definitions of the two elements are required.

We define buying proposal as *all the verbal and visual components of advertising that correspond to product attributes, price, brand name, country-of-origin, and the benefits of product consumption.* These elements are vital for consumer's cognitive evaluations of product value. In contrast, we define creative presentation as *all the visual and verbal components of advertising that surround the buying proposal to attract attention or interest consumers or influence their feelings toward the product.*

The distinction scheme of dual elements (buying proposal and creative presentation) of international advertising is similar to that of the dual process model of persuasion. The dual process models of persuasion, the Elaboration Likelihood Model (ELM) and the Heuristic Systematic Model (HSM), suggest that two concurrent modes of information processing exist (Chaiken 1980; Petty and Caccioppo 1979). In this research, we define buying proposal as being a narrower concept than message content. We exclude such elements of message content as foreign word, humor, and life-style from buying proposal but include them in the category of creative presentation of international advertising. We also posit that creative presentation does not include non-ad inducements such as consensus information (i.e., the opinion of others), but heuristic cues in dual process model of persuasion do include non-ad inducements. Heuristic cues in the dual process model of persuasion are defined to include such elements of advertising as background settings, music, model, artifacts, and non-advertising elements such as consensus information. Thus, creative presentation includes some portion of heuristic cues (such as background settings, music, model, artifacts) as well as some portion of message content (such as foreign word, life-style, humor, etc.), but it does not include non-ad inducements.

According to attitude toward the ad model, it is critical to distinguish between and separately measure cognitive evaluations of the ad and affective responses toward the ad in assessing consumer attitudes toward the ad. Also, attitude toward an advertisement (Aad) is understood as a significant mediator of the relationship between consumer's cognitive and affective responses and brand attitude. Correspondingly, when consumers are exposed to a foreign ad, they will execute cognitive evaluations and affective responses to buying proposal and creative presentation, and these in turn will affect their attitude toward the foreign ad. Based on the dual process model of persuasion, attitude toward the ad model, and our definition of dual elements of international advertising, we hypothesize the following:

Hypothesis 1: Consumer's responses to the buying proposal and creative presentation of a foreign advertisement have a direct effect on their attitude toward the foreign advertisement.

Effect of Country-of-Origin Perception on Ad Response

Country-of-origin studies (e.g., Agbonifoh and Elimimian 1999; Ahmed and d Astous 1995; Ahmed, d Astous, and Lemire 1997; Chao and Gupta 1995; Gurhan-Canli and Maheswaran 2000; Insch and Mcbride 1998; Li and Dant 1997; Li, Murray, and Scott 2000) have shown that consumers use country-of-origin information to evaluate products and that country-of-origin influences evaluations by signaling product quality. Marketing researchers have made many attempts to ascertain whether a manifestation of the country-of-origin enhances the sales prospects of a product. In domestic and international advertising, the "made in" concept has established itself as one of the clearly identifiable strategies employed by companies of many different countries (Head 1988). The cases in which advertising exploits the connection with the country-of-origin in order to enhance a product's appeal have been cited frequently (Waldron 1982; Whalen 1984; Yavas and Alpay 1986). Head posited that the "made in" advertising slogan brings to the attention of a foreign audience positive and usually stereotypical attributes of another country and imbues the product originating from that country with these image-enhancing qualities. He also showed that deployment of the country-of-origin as a selling point derives its justification not just from humorous stereotyping, but also from allusion to a particular expertise which is associated with the foreign country and which thereby instills confidence in the product.

As discussed earlier, the buying proposal is the sales point of the seller, consisting of the elements of foreign advertising that correspond to product attributes, price, brand name, and benefits of product consumption. Consumers use country-of-origin as stereotypical information in evaluating the product depicted by foreign advertisements. Accordingly, consumer's country-of-origin perceptions will primarily affect their responses to the buying proposal of a foreign advertisement. Consumer's country-of-origin perceptions are stereotypical information on which they base evaluations of product quality; so it is directed toward the theme, "buy a product made in a particular country" rather than toward other secondary inducement components (creative presentation) of a foreign advertisement. Based on this reasoning, we state the following hypothesis:

Hypothesis 2: Consumers' country-of-origin perceptions primarily affect their responses to the buying proposal of a foreign advertisement. That is, consumers who have positive (negative) perceptions about a particular product category made in a certain country will show favorable (unfavorable) responses to the buying proposal of a foreign ad.

Effects of Consumer Ethnocentrism on Ad Responses

Shimp and Sharma (1987) noted that "consumer ethnocentrism gives the individual a sense of identity, feelings of belonging, and, most importantly, an understanding of what purchase behavior is acceptable or unacceptable to the in-group" (p. 280). They showed that consumer ethnocentrism correlates with patriotism, politico-economic conservatism, and dogmatism. Sharma, Shimp, and Shin (1995) showed that consumer ethnocentrism is positively correlated with patriotic and conservative attitudes but negatively correlated with cultural openness. Accordingly, a consumer who has a high ethnocentric tendency will be dogmatic and not open to foreign culture, so s/he will have generally unfavorable attitudes toward foreign countries and culture. Some studies (Durvasula, Craig, and Netemeyer 1997; Klein and Ettenson 1999) examined and compared consumer ethnocentrism across countries and showed significant difference between nations.

Head (1988) demonstrated the negative impact of touching the consumers' xenophobic nerve in his description of British responses to a foreign ad: "Where the Audi commercial depicted the *'Vorsprung durch Technik'* slogan at the end, the sketch at the appropriate point displays in wobbly orthography the words *'Deutschland uber Alles.'* In this instance, the Audi catch-phrase is seen unequivocally as a provocation, for its exploitation of 'Germany' as a symbol of superiority is equated with the *'Herrenvolk'* ideology of the Third Reich. . . . It is as though the advertisements for Audi, by implying that British cars are not up to the competition from yesterday's defeated enemy, have touched upon a raw xenophobic nerve" (p. 250).

Consumer ethnocentrism derives from the more general construct of ethnocentrism, which is defined as people viewing their in-group as central, as possessing proper standards, of behavior, and as offering protection against apparent threats from out-groups (Brislin 1993). As Klein, Ettenson, and Morris (1998, p. 90) noted out, "Shimp and Sharma (1987) apply ethnocentrism to the study of marketing and consumer behavior and have coined the term "consumer ethnocentric tendencies" to represent beliefs held by consumers regarding the appropriateness and morality of purchasing foreign made products." According to Shimp and Sharma's definition and operationalization of consumer ethnocentrism, one might argue that it could affect both creative presentation and buying proposal of international advertising. However, when the roles of consumer ethnocentrism and country of origin perception on consumer processing of international advertising are considered simultaneously, the impact of consumer ethnocentrism is likely to be directed more to the creative presentation rather than the buying proposal. That is, it is more likely to influence consumer's response to the visual and verbal components of advertising that surround the buying proposal to attract attention or interest consumers or influence their feelings toward the product rather than buying proposal (the verbal and visual components of advertising that correspond to product attributes, price, brand name, country-of-origin, and the benefits of product consumption). Even though the nature of consumer ethnocentrism has the possibility to influence both consumer response to the creative presentation and buying proposal, because consumer's country of origin perception affects overwhelmingly consumer response to the buying proposal, the influence of consumer ethnocentrism to consumer response to the buying proposal is likely to be suffocated. Based on the above, we put forth the following hypothesis:

Hypothesis 3: Consumer's ethnocentrism primarily affect their responses to the creative presentation of a foreign advertisement. That is, consumers who have high (low) ethnocentric tendencies will show unfavorable (favorable) responses to the creative presentation of a foreign advertisement.

Mediating Roles of Consumer Responses to the Buying Proposal and Creative Presentation

Up to this point, we have hypothesized about the direct effects of consumer's responses to the buying proposal and creative presentation of a foreign advertisement on their attitude toward the ad (Hypothesis 1). We also hypothesized that there would be positive effects of consumer's country-of-origin perceptions on their responses to the buying proposal (Hypothesis 2), and negative effects of consumer ethnocentrism on their responses to the creative presentation (Hypothesis 3). Based on the above, we propose the following hypothesis:

Hypothesis 4: Consumer's responses to the buying proposal and creative presentation of a foreign advertisement mediate the effects of consumer's country-of-origin perceptions and consumer ethnocentrism on their attitude toward the ad.

METHODOLOGY

In the experimental study, South Korean consumers were exposed to selected foreign (American, German, French, and Italian) ads appearing in South Korea. The reason of choosing South Korean consumers is that foreign advertisements in foreign cultural context are pervasive in this country. It examines subject's responses to the creative presentation and buying proposal of the foreign ads, and attitudes toward the foreign ads. Individual subject's degrees of consumer ethnocentrism, and country-of-origin perceptions were surveyed in two separate sessions.

For the model estimation, we employed structural equation modeling. Goldberger (1973) considered three situations in which structural equations provide relevant information that regression parameters fail to give: (1) when the observed variables contain measurement errors and the interesting relationship is among the true or attenuated variables, (2) when there is interdependence or simultaneous causation among the observed response variables, and (3) when important explanatory variables have not been observed. Like many substantive research problems in the social and behavioral sciences, our research problems fall under these categories, so we used structural equation modeling.

Operationalization of Constructs

Consumer Ethnocentrism

Consumer ethnocentrism is measured using the CETSCALE, that was developed and validated in former studies (Netemeyer, Durvasula, and Lichtenstein 1991; Shimp and Sharma 1987). Separate studies provided support for the reliability and convergent and discriminant validity of the 17-item CETSCALE. Studies also assessed the psychometric properties and nomological validity of the CETSCALE across different countries. The results suggest that the CETSCALE is a reliable measure across different countries and that it affords evidence of validity as well (Netemeyer, Durvasula, and Lichtenstein 1991).

Country-of-Origin Perception

Country-of-origin research focuses on consumer's opinions regarding the relative qualities of goods and services produced in various countries. We coin a terminology, "country-of-origin perception," that denotes consumer's perceptions regarding the relative qualities of goods and services produced in various countries. We operationalize this construct by asking subjects to indicate their opinions about critical product attributes of each of eight product categories (refrigerator, automobile, cognac, leather sofa, cosmetics, kids' clothes, steam iron, and dishwasher). The batteries of critical product attributes of each product category are selected based upon product rating items used in the *Consumer Reports* and in previous research. For example, the attributes of performance, noise level, and energy efficiency are selected for refrigerators, and the attributes of technology, prestige, and reliability are selected for automobiles.

The country of origin perception scales for each of the eight product categories were composed of three items. The scale's internal consistency reliability was assessed. Coefficient alpha for the eight product categories ranges from 0.87 to 0.96. Test-retest reliability was also administered separated by a two-week period. The correlation between these two period ranges from 0.83 to 0.91. Both sets of results indicate that the country of origin perception scales are reliable index of consumer's perception of country of origin of a specific product.

Responses to Creative Presentation and Buying Proposal

Consumers are asked to list their thoughts about creative presentation, buying proposal, and overall evaluation of each ad after they see the foreign ads. The listed thoughts are coded into three categories: thoughts on creative presentation (TCP), thoughts on buying proposal (TBP), and thoughts on overall ad (TAD). Each of the thoughts is coded to have valences of positive, negative, or neutral. Our coding scheme is built upon previous research on protocol responses to advertising (Cacioppo et al. 1981; Greenwald 1968; Higie and Spiggle 1989; Wright 1973).

Two trained judges and the author coded the listed thoughts. The interjudge reliability was assessed by the percentage of agreement between each set of two judges. In the marketing research literature, there is no accepted standard for evaluating the reliability of coded data even if multiple judges are used. The most commonly used measure of interjudge reliability is the percentage of agreement between two or more judges (cf. Bettman and Park 1980; Cohen 1960; Zwick 1988). Kassarjian (1977) suggested 85 percent as the minimum interjudge reliability.

Each of the coded thoughts of the same category is calculated to result in a total valence. That is, for the same thought category, the number of positive thoughts minus negative thoughts becomes the numerator. The number of total thoughts (positive, negative, and neutral) becomes the denominator. For example, if a subject listed two positive, one negative, and one neutral thought on creative presentation, the total valence of response to creative presentation is $(2 - 1)/(2 + 1 + 1) = 0.25$. This method is more valid than the simple addition method because it allows us to ascertain the number of neutral thoughts (Hamilton, Hunter, and Boster 1993). For example, with the simple addition method, a subject's response of two positive, one negative, and one neutral thought is construed to be the same as that of two positive and one negative thought.

Attitude Toward the Ad

Subjects are asked to rate their attitude toward the ad on a three-item index–favorable/unfavorable, positive/negative, good/bad. These attitude measures were commonly used in previous research (Burke and Edell 1989;

Holbrook and Batra 1987). Several scales are reversed to prevent the halo effect.

Stimulus Ads

Magazine ads currently existing in South Korea were used. These stimuli ads satisfied the following requirements: (1) They advertise a brand whose country of origin is foreign, (2) creative presentations of the ads contain a foreign flavor, that is, foreign model, artifacts, scenery, words, etc., and (3) most consumers have some knowledge about the culture of the countries in question; that is, the origin countries are large countries. Consumers may know the country-of-origin of some of the brands but not others, prior to being exposed to the stimulus ads. The majority of foreign ads in South Korea usually manifest the country-of-origin of the products. We inserted country-of-origin clarification into the ads that did not have one. We did the manipulation check at the final stage of the experiment to determine whether subjects recognized countries-of-origin of the products featured in the stimuli foreign ads.

Considering international trade and political relationships with South Korea, we chose four major Western countries–the U.S., Germany, France, and Italy–that market and advertise extensively in South Korea.

Subjects

Subjects were adult consumers who reside in Seoul, South Korea. They were employees working at three companies, i.e., Samsung Group, Hanwha Group, Dongyang Group affiliated with "Jaebol Groups" (Korean conglomerates) and high school teachers at Dongdeuk High School. The author commissioned four assistants within the institutions to recruit the subjects and administer the surveys.

Two hundred fifty-one subjects out of 300 potential subjects contacted agreed to participate in the experiments. We excluded twelve subjects who did not recognize (answer) countries-of-origin of the products featured in the ads correctly. As a result, we collected the data from 239 subjects.

Regarding the appropriate sample size for structural equation modeling, Anderson and Gerbing (1984, 1988) found that a sample size of 150 will usually be sufficient to obtain a converged and proper solution for measurement models with three or more indicators per factor. Boomsma (1985, 1996) and Tanaka (1987) suggested that sample sizes of 100 are strong lower bounds when considering maximum likelihood estimation of structural equation models, and they suggested samples of 200 or more.

We traced the identification of the subjects through the entire sessions by letting the author's four assistants note the subjects' names on the back cover page right after they picked up the questionnaires from the two sessions. The four assistants had initially contacted the subjects when soliciting people to join the experiments, and therefore they knew the subjects' names. After we completed the two sessions of the experiment, we bundled two pieces of questionnaires as one set. The author later codified the sets of questionnaires using sequential numbers to facilitate data analyses. The data were collected during June-July of 1998.

Procedure

We used extreme caution in preparing the questionnaires, because, while this study was originated and designed in the U.S., subject's behavioral data would be collected in a non-English-speaking foreign country, South Korea. Questionnaires were translated into Korean and back to English by separate bilingual experts. To validate the Korean version of the questionnaire, we conducted a pilot study with five Korean graduate students at New England province. Questionnaires were simplified as much as possible. The instructions were revised based upon the feedback from the subjects of the pilot study in order to get consistent responses from the subjects and facilitate survey administration in South Korea.

First Session

Subjects were informed that they would be participating in a "consumer's beliefs study." Subject's degrees of ethnocentrism were measured using the CETSCALE developed by Shimp and Sharma (1987) as in Study 1. Subjects were asked to note their reactions to the 17-item CETSCALE on 7-point Likert scales. Subject's country-of-origin perceptions were also measured. Measurement scales for country-of-origin perception of each product category were devised by the author in accordance with previous research and the product rating criteria used in the Consumer Report. Subjects were asked to note their perceptions on 7-point semantic scales.

Second Session

In the second session, which took place two weeks after the first, subjects were informed that they would be participating in an "advertising study." To give subjects the notion that the second session was not related to the first session, we used different fonts and colored papers for the questionnaires of all two sessions. To check subjects' recognition of the study objectives we included the question about their notion of the study objectives.

Each subject was given a booklet containing four stimulus ads. The instructions were: "In this booklet you will find several full color print advertisements for foreign brand products. Please note that all the print ads in this booklet are in 'rough' condition. We are interested in your reactions toward these ads. We would like you to examine each ad in this booklet just as you would if you had come across in a magazine. Take as much or as little time as you like to examine each ad. Then turn the page and respond to the instructions provided. Remember that there are no 'right' or 'wrong' responses, we are only interested in your honest responses. For the validity of this research, please be frank." Each ad promoted a product made in a different foreign countries. After subjects were exposed to each ad, they were asked to write down on a lined blank sheet all the thoughts that went through their mind as they examined the ad, one thought per line. After listing thoughts, they were also asked to express their attitude toward the ad on seven-point semantic scales.

ANALYSIS AND RESULTS

Coding

Coding of the response protocols was done by three judges—the first author and two independent, trained coders who were blind to the research objectives and hypotheses. Almost all the responses on each line were distinct thoughts, as per the instructions. However, some responses included two thoughts. They were separated into individual thoughts through discussion among judges and coded independently by the three judges.

In total 5,188 thoughts were listed. The interjudge agreement was on average 94.3 percent. The agreement between the author and Judge A, the author and Judge B, and Judges A and B were 94.6, 95.1, and 93.2 percent, respectively. Disagreements were resolved by a two-step process. First, Judge A and B's coding were adopted when they did not agree with the author's coding. Second, Judges A and B resolved the remaining discrepancies after each judge was shown the other's initial coding.

Each thought was coded into thought on creative presentation, thought on buying proposal, and thought on overall ad evaluation. Each thought was given a valence of positive, negative, or neutral. Consequently, each subject's responses toward creative presentation and buying proposal were assessed in the following manner: For each thought category, the total number of positive thoughts minus negative thoughts became the numerator. The number of total thoughts (positive, negative, and neutral) in each thought category became the denominator.

Manipulation Check

We first checked the manipulation of the countries-of-origin of the products featured in the ads. We had included the question, "Which country was the product made in?" on the last page of the second session's questionnaire. 97.6% of the subjects knew the correct countries-of-origin of all the products featured in the ads. We also checked subject's awareness of the study objectives. We had included the question, "What do you think is the purpose of this research?" on the last page of the second session's questionnaire. No subjects grasped our genuine purposes.

Structural Equation System

There is some dispute regarding the comparative advantages of the one-step and two-step approaches in structural equation modeling research. The one-step approach, suggested by Fornell and Yi (1992), is to analyze structural and measurement models simultaneously. The two-step approach, suggested by Anderson and Gerbing (1988, 1990), is to estimate the measurement model prior to the estimation of structural model. Anderson and Gerbing (1988, p. 411) noted several advantages of the two-step approach as follows: "We contend that there is much to gain in theory testing and assessment of construct validity from separate estimation of the measurement model prior to the simultaneous estimation of the measurement and structural submodels. The measurement model provides a confirmatory assessment of convergent validity and discriminant validity (Campbell and Fiske 1959). Given acceptable convergent and discriminant validities, the test of the structural model then constitutes a confirmatory assessment of nomological validity" (Campbell 1960; Cronbach and Meehl 1955). Thus, we adopted the two-step approach in this study.

Measurement Model

Three procedures were used to test the measurement properties of the model, using LISREL analysis (Joreskog and Sorbom 1993). First, in order to assess unidimensionality, each construct in the model was analyzed using confirmatory factor analysis type measurement models separately, and the fit of the indicators to the construct was assessed. The fit indices for all the constructs measured by multiple indicators were perfect, except for the construct of consumer ethnocentrism.

For consumer ethnocentrism, results of the single construct measurement model were poor. The normed χ^2 index indicated a poor level of fit, as did the RMSEA and other fit indices (normed $\chi^2 = 6.25$, RMSEA = .27, GFI = .89, AGFI =.81, CFI = .84). Because the CETSCALE is a validated measure, the scale was not modified to increase the level of fit. Instead, the 17 CETSCALE questions were aggregated and the average was used as a single indicator of consumer ethnocentrism which is consistent with the method used by Klein,

Ettenson, and Morris (1998). Because it is hard to ensure that single indicators are perfectly measured, we fixed the error variances at $(1 - \text{Cronbach } \alpha) \times s^2$ of the index of the CETSCALE items for consumer ethnocentrism (Hair, Anderson, Tatham, and Black 1995; Joreskog and Sorbom 1993, p. 153). As a result, the variance of consumer ethnocentrism was fixed at 1.99.

Responses to the creative presentation (Rcp) and buying proposal (Rbp) were represented by thought on creative presentation and thought on buying proposal. Although no replicate measures are available for these constructs, the indicators must be considered fallible. A reliability of .85 was therefore assumed for thought on creative presentation and thought on buying proposal, on the grounds that a typical value of .85 is a better assumption than an arbitrary value of 1.00 (Joreskog and Sorbom 1996). As a result, the variances were fixed at 2.09 and 1.89 for responses to the creative presentation and buying proposal.

Second, the goodness of fit of the full measurement model was assessed. All the fit indices, except the normed χ^2 (RMSEA, GFI, AGFI, and CFI) indicate a good level of model fit (Normed Chi-square = 3.14, RMSEA = .072, GFI = .95, AGFI = .91, CFI = .97). The χ^2 statistic has been found to be subject to bias due to sample size (Bagozzi 1981; Gerbing and Anderson 1992). As a result, the normed χ^2 (χ^2/df) is recommended when sample size is greater than 200 (Carmines and McIver 1981; Hair, Anderson, Tatham, and Black 1995; Klein, Ettenson, and Morris 1998). Ratios below 2 or 3 have been recommended as indicating an acceptable level of fit. RMSEA lower than .08 and GFI, AGFI, and CFI above .90 indicate acceptable fit (Bentler and Bonnet 1980; Bollen 1989; Hair, Anderson, Tatham, and Black 1995; Joreskog and Sorbom 1982). Third, each construct was tested for construct reliability. The reliability coefficients (Cronbach αs) of all constructs were bigger than 0.85.

Structural Model

The results of the LISREL analysis for the structural model indicate that our hypothetical model achieved high levels of fit. The normed χ^2 = 1.96, the RMSEA = .01, the GFI = .99, the AGFI = .96, and the CFI = .99.

Since multiple models can fit a given covariance matrix, we needed to test alternative models and demonstrate a significant decrease in fit when going from the established model to an alternative model as indicated by a significant increase in χ^2 (Anderson and Gerbing 1988). Two alternative models were tested for each case: (1) the path from consumer ethnocentrism (CE) to responses to the buying proposal (Rbp) was added; and (2) the path from CE to responses to the creative presentation (Rcp) and the path from country-of-origin perception (COOP) to Rbp were removed and the path from CE to Rbp and the path from COOP to Rcp were added. All two alternative models showed a significant increase in χ^2 from the hypothesized model, an increase in RMSEA, and a decrease in the GFI, the AGFI, and the CFI.

Hypothesis 1: Effects of Consumer's Responses to the Buying Proposal and Creative Presentation on Their Aad. The effects of consumer's responses to the buying proposal (Rbp) and creative presentation (Rcp) of a foreign ad on their attitude toward the ad was assessed by the paths estimated by structural equation modeling analysis. Figure 2 shows the coefficients and p values of the paths in structural models. As predicted by Hypothesis 1, the standardized solution paths from Rcp to Aad (.90, p < .05) and from Rbp to Aad (.89, p < .05) were significant and positive. Hypothesis 1 was supported.

Hypothesis 2: Positive Effect of Consumer's Country-of-Origin Perceptions on Their Responses to the Buying Proposal. To analyze the positive effect of consumer's country-of-origin perceptions on their responses to the buying proposal of a foreign ad, we investigated the causal relationship by structural equation modeling. The effect of consumer's country-of-origin perceptions were significantly positive on Rbp (.57, p < .05) as shown in Figure 2. Thus, Hypothesis 2 was supported.

Hypothesis 3: Negative Effect of Consumer Ethnocentrism on Their Responses to the Creative Presentation. To assess the negative effect of consumer ethnocentrism on their responses to the creative presentation of a

FIGURE 2. Structural Model

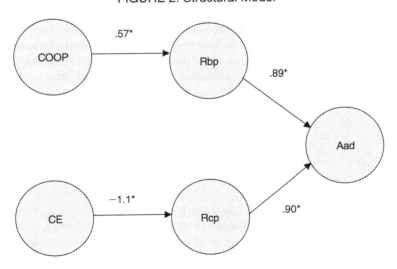

Note: * p < 0.05

foreign ad, we also investigated the causal relationship by structural equation modeling. In the hypothesized structural model, the path from CE to Rcp was significantly negative (-1.1, $p < .05$). The result support Hypothesis 3.

Hypothesis 4: Roles of Consumer's Responses to the Buying Proposal and Culture-Related Creative Presentation as Mediators of Aad. The roles of consumer's responses to the buying proposal and creative presentation of a foreign ad as mediators of Aad were also assessed. As predicted by Hypothesis 4, the path from CE to Rcp (-1.1, $p < .05$) was significantly negative. Moreover, the path from Rcp to Aad (.90, $p < .05$) was significantly positive. Furthermore, the path from COOP to Rbp (.57, $p < .05$) and from Rbp to Aad (.89, $p < .05$) were also significantly positive. Thus, we could confirm the mediating roles of Rcp and Rbp. Thus, Hypothesis 4 was supported.

CONCLUSIONS AND MANAGERIAL IMPLICATIONS

This research examines the impacts of consumer's two cross-national individual difference variables–country-of-origin perception and consumer ethnocentrism–on their responses and attitudes toward foreign advertisements. Empirical analysis of the hypothetical model through structural equation modeling yields supportive results: negative effects of consumer's ethnocentrism on their responses to the creative presentation of international advertising, and positive effects of consumer's country-of-origin perceptions on their responses to the buying proposal of international advertising.

The research has managerial implications that may shed light on the standardization versus localization debate in international advertising (and marketing) strategy (Cavusgil, Zou, and Naidu 1993; Samiee and Roth 1992; Szymanski, Bharadwaj, and Varadarajan 1993). The rationale of the standardization strategy is summarized by Szymanski, Bharadwaj, and Varadarajan (1993, p. 10) as follows: "Sales can be increased by developing a consistent image of the product across national market; and costs can be lowered by pooling production activities across countries, moving production to low-cost locations without redefining the production process, and capturing the economies associated with formulating and implementing a single marketing plan." They also summarize the rationale of the localization strategy as follows: "Because few markets are exactly alike, some adaptation of marketing program is necessary to ensure that buyer needs are satisfied effectively and sales maximized."

However, as Onkvisit and Shaw (1999, p. 19) has noted, "Many scholars who are involved in the three decade-old debate of effectiveness of standardization versus adaptation of international advertising have used anecdotes to buttress their point of view. Arguments need to be grounded in fact rather than intuition . . . Isolated incidents, without proper control mechanisms, are highly suspect and can be easily twisted. It is unreasonable to merely cite a particular company's campaign as an example of the failure or success of a standardized tactic present, the available empirical data, although plentiful, deal with the ineffectiveness of standardized advertising only in an indirect manner."

The results of this study provide some direct and conclusive evidence to establish a cause and effect relationship. Thus, it may provide international marketing managers some knowledge regarding when and how much they need to standardize the marketing program. Further, this study suggests some guidelines to determine the components and degree of localization of international advertising. It provides answers to the following questions: What elements of international advertising should be localized to appeal to foreign consumers? For which countries' target consumers should international ads be localized or standardized? If target market consumer's country-of-origin images of a product were weak, would it be strategically desirable to adapt a product and its advertising so that it could be promoted as different from, rather than typical of, that country's products?

International marketing managers should clearly research the target market consumers' degree of consumer ethnocentrism and perception of country of origin regarding the product category. For example, the Japanese automobile marketers planning to enter the Korean market should examine the degree of consumer ethnocentrism of Korean consumers. They also need to research on how Korean consumers perceive the automobiles made in Japan, the United States, Germany, and other competitor's origin country. Based on these, the international marketers may use the standardization-localization strategy grid composed of target market consumer's ethnocentrism and country-of-origin perceptions as depicted in Figure 3.

Four alternative strategies of international advertising are provided. Firstly, full standardization strategy (standardized CP and standardized BP) is likely to be preferable if target market consumer's degrees of ethnocentrism are low

FIGURE 3. Standardization-Localization Strategy Grid

	Low CE	High CE
Good COOP	Full Standardization Strategy Standardized CP Standardized BP	Partial Localization Strategy (A) Localized CP Standardized BP
Bad COOP	Partial Localization Strategy (B) Standardized CP Localized BP	Full Localization Strategy Localized CP Localized BP

and country-of-origin perceptions are good. That is, in the case of Japanese automobile company entering to the U.S. market, if American consumer's degree of ethnocentrism is relatively low and they perceive Japanese automobile as excellent, the Japanese automobile marketer may use a standardized advertisement copy in the U.S. that is the same as used in home market. Secondly, full localization (customization, adaptation, and modification) strategy (localized CP and localized BP) is likely to be preferable if target market consumers' degrees of ethnocentrism are high and country-of-origin perceptions are bad. That is, in the case of Korean automobile company entering to the Chinese market, if Chinese consumers' degree of ethnocentrism is relatively high and they perceive Korean automobile as poor or not valuable, the Korean automobile marketer may use an advertisement copy that contains creative presentations and buying proposals appropriate in the Chinese market. Thirdly, partial localization strategy (A) (localized CP and standardized BP) is likely to be preferable if target market consumers' degree of ethnocentrism is relatively high but their country-of-origin perception is good. That is, in the case of Japanese automobile company entering to the Korean market, if Korean consumers' degree of ethnocentrism is relatively high but they perceive Japanese automobile as good and valuable, the Japanese automobile marketer may use an advertisement copy that contains localized creative presentations appropriate in Korean market and standardized buying proposals to achieve global positioning. Lastly, partial localization strategy (B) (standardized CP and localized BP) is likely to be preferable if target market consumer's degree of ethnocentrism is relatively low but their country-of-origin perception is poor. That is, in the case of Korean automobile company entering to the U.S. market, if American consumer's degree of ethnocentrism is relatively low but they perceive Korean automobile as poor, the Korean automobile marketer may use an advertisement copy that contains standardized creative presentations to achieve global image and save ad production cost and localized buying proposals to minimize the negative effect of county of origin affiliation.

REFERENCES

Aaker, Jennifer and Durairaj Maheswaran (1996), "The Effect of Cultural Orientation and Cue Diagnosticity on Processing and Product Evaluations," Working Paper, No. 257, Marketing Studies Center, UCLA.

Agbonifoh, Barnabas A. and Jonathan U. Elimimian (1999), "Attitudes of Developing Countries Towards Country-of-Origin Products in An Era of Multiple Brands," *Journal of International Consumer Marketing*, 11 (4), 97-116.

Ahmed, Sadrudin A. and d Astous Alain (1995), "Comparison of Country-of-Origin Effects on Household and Organizational Consumers," *European Journal of Marketing*, 29 (3), 35-41.

_____, and Simon Lemire (1997), "Country-of-Origin Effects in the U.S. and Canada: Implications for the Marketing of Products Made in Mexico," *Journal of International Consumer Marketing*, 10 (1), 73-92.

Anderson, J.C. and D.W. Gerbing (1984), "The Effect of Sampling Error on Convergence, Improper Solutions, and Goodness-of-Fit Indices for Maximum Likelihood Confirmatory Factor Analysis," *Psychometrika*, 49, 155-73.

Bagozzi, Richard P, Nancy Wong, and Youjae Yi (1997), "On the Representation of Affect in Interdependent and Independent Cultures," *Advances in Consumer Research*, Vol. 24.

Batra, Rajeev and Michael L. Ray (1986), "Affective Responses Mediating Acceptance of Advertising," *Journal of Consumer Research*, 13 (September), 234-49.

Bentler, P.M. and Douglas G. Bonett (1980), "Significance Tests and Goodness of Fit in the Analysis of Covariance Structures," *Psychological Bulletin*, 88, 588-606.

Boomsma, Anne (1985), "Nonconvergence, Improper Solutions, and Starting Values in LISREL Maximum Likelihood Estimation," *Psychometrika*, 50 (2), 229-42.

Brislin, Richard (1993), *Understanding Culture's Influence on Behavior*, Orlando, FL: Jarcourt Brace Jovanivich.

Cavusgil, S. Tamer, Shaoming Zou, and G.M. Naidu (1993), "Product and Promotion Adaptation in Export Ventures: An Empirical Investigation," *Journal of International Business Studies*, Third Quarter, 479-506.

Chaiken, Shelly, and Durairaj Maheswaran (1994), "Heuristic Processing Can Bias Systematic Processing: Effects of Source Credibility, Argument Ambiguity. and Task Importance on Evaluation Judgments," *Journal of Personality and Social Psychology*, 66, 460-73.

Chao, Paul (1998), "Impact of Country of Origin Dimensions on Product Quality and Design Quality," *Journal of Business Research*, 42 (1), 1-6 (1998).

_____ and Pola B. Gupta (1995), "Information Search and Efficiency of Consumer Choice of New Cars: Country-of-Origin Effects," *International Marketing Review*, 12 (6), 47-59.

Dunn, S. Watson (1976), "Effect of National Identity on Multinational Promotional Strategy in Europe," *Journal of Marketing*, 50-7.

Durvasula, Srinivas, J. Craig Andrews, and Richard G. Netemeyer (1997), "A Cross-Cultural Comparison of Consumer Ethnocentrism in the United States and Russia," *Journal of International Consumer Marketing*, 9 (4), 73-93.

Dzever, Sam and Pascale Quester (1999), "Country of Origin Effects on Purchasing Agent's Product Perceptions: An Australian Perspective, *Industrial Marketing Management*, 28 (2), 165-175.

Ettenson, R. "Brand Name and Country of Origin Effects in the Emerging Market Economies of Russia, Poland, and Hungary," *International Marketing Review*, 10 (5), 14-36.

Etzel, Michael J. and Bruce J. Walker (1974), "Advertising Strategy for Foreign Products," *Journal of Advertising Research*, 14 (June), 41-4.

Fornell, C. and Y. Yi (1992), "Assumptions of the Two-Step Approach to Latent Variable Modeling," *Sociological Methods and Research*, Vol. 20, 291-320.

Gerbing, David W. and James C. Anderson (1992), "Monte Carlo Evaluations of Goodness of Fit Indices for Structural Equation Models," *Sociological Methods and Research*, 21, 132-60.

Goldberger, A.S. (1973), "Structural Equation Models: An Overview" in *Structural Equation Models in the Social Sciences*, A.S.Goldberg and O.D. Duncan eds., New York: Seminar Press.

Gronhaug, Kjell and Morten Heide (1992), "Stereotyping in Country Advertising," *European Journal of Marketing*, 26 (5), 56-67.

Gurhan-Canli, Zeynep and Durairaj Maheswaran (2000), "Determinants of Country-of-Origin Evaluations," *Journal of Consumer Research*, 27 (1), 96-108.

Hafhill, D.S. (1980), "Multinational Marketing Strategy: Implications for Attitudes Toward Country of Origin," *Management International Review*, 20 (4), 26-30.

Han, C. Min (1988), "The Role of Consumer Patriotism in the Choice of Domestic Versus Foreign Products," *Journal of Advertising Research*, 28 (June/July), 25-32.

Head, David (1988), "Advertising Slogans and the "Made-ln" Concept," *International Journal of Advertising*, 7, 237-252.

Higie, Robin A. and Susan Spiggle (1989), "Protocol Responses to Advertisements: A Coding Scheme," *Winter Marketing Educator's Conference Proceedings*, Chicago: American Marketing Association.

Hong, Sung-Tai and Robert S. Wyer (1989), "Effects of Country-of-Origin and Product-Attribute Information on Product Evaluation: An Information Processing Perspective," *Journal of Consumer Research*, 16 (September), 175-87.

Insch, Gary S. and J. Brad McBride (1998), "Decomposing the Country-of-Origin Construct: An Empirical Test of Country of Design, Country of Parts, and Country of Assembly," *Journal of International Consumer Marketing*, 10 (4), 69-91.

Jain, Subhash C. (1989), "Standardization of International Marketing Strategy: Some Research Hypotheses," *Journal of Marketing*, 53 (January), 70-9.

Joreskog, Karl G. and Dag Sorbom (1982), "Recent Developments in Structural Equation Modeling," *Journal of Marketing Research*, 19, 404-16.

Kanso, Ali (1992), "International Advertising Strategies: Global Commitment to Local Vision," *Journal of Advertising Research*, Jan/Feb, 10-14.

Kaynak, Erdener and Tamer Cavusgil (1983), "Consumer Attitudes Towards Products of Foreign Origin: Do They Vary Across Product Classes?" *International Journal of Advertising*, 2, 147-57.

Killough, James (1978), "Improved Payoffs From Transnational Advertising, *Harvard Business Review*, July-August 1978, 102-10.

Kim, Chung Koo and Jay Young Chung (1997), "Brand Popularity, Country Image, and Market Share: An Empirical Study," *Journal of International Business Studies*, 28 (2), 361-386.

Klein, Jill G. and Richard Ettenson (1999), "Consumer Animosity and Consumer Ethnocentrism: An Analysis of Unique Antecedents," *Journal of International Consumer Marketing*, 11 (4), 5-24.

_____ and M. Morris (1998), "The Animosity Model of Foreign Product Purchase: An Empirical Test in the People's Republic of China," *Journal of Marketing*, January.

Li, Zhan G. and Rajiv P. Dant (1997), "Dimensions of Product Quality and Country-of-Origin Effects Research," *Journal of International Consumer Marketing*, 10 (1), 93-114.

_____, William Murray, and Don Scott (2000), "Global Sourcing, Multiple Country-of-Origin Facets, and Consumer Reactions," *Journal of Business Research*, 47 (2), 121-133.

Maheswaran, Durairaj (1994), "Country of Origin as a Stereotype: Effects of Consumer Expertise and Attribute Strength on Product Evaluation," *Journal of Consumer Research*, 21 (September), 354-65.

Mooij, Marieke K. and Warren J. Keegan (1991), *Advertising Worldwide*, UK: Prentice Hall International.

Moon, Byeong-Joon (1995), "The Impact of Consumer's Acculturation Attitude on Responses to Multinational Advertisements," *Marketing Theory and Practice: Toward the 21st Century*, KMA-AMA Joint Conference.

_____ (1996), "The Roles of Consumer Ethnocentricity and Attitude Toward a Foreign Culture in Processing Foreign Country-of-Origin Advertisements," *Advances in Consumer Research*, Vol. 23, eds. Kim P. Corfman and G. Lynch, Jr., Provo, Utah: Association for Consumer Research, 436-9.

Mueller, Barbara (1991), "An Analysis of Information Content in Standardized vs. Specialized Multinational Advertisements," *Journal of International Business Studies*, First Quarter, 23-39.

_____ (1992), "Standardization vs. Specialization: An Examination of Westernization in Japanese Advertising," *Journal of Advertising Research*, 32 (January/February), 15-24.

Narayana, C.L. (1981), "Aggregate Image of American and Japanese Products: Implications on International Marketing," *Columbia Journal of World Business*, 16 (2), 31-5.

Nebenzahl, Israel D., Eugene D. Jaffe, and Shlomo I. Lampert (1997), "Toward a Theory of Country Image Effect on Product Evaluation," *Management International Review*, 37 (1), 27-49.

Netemeyer, Richard G., Srinivas Durvasula, and Donald R. Lichtenstein (1991), "A Cross-National Assessment of the Reliability and Validity of the CETSCALE," *Journal of Marketing Research*, 28 (August), 320-7.

Onkvisit, Sak and John J. Shaw (1999), "Standardized International Advertising: Some Research Issues and Implications," *Journal of Advertising Research*, 19-24.

Samiee, Saeed and Kendall Roth (1992), "The Influence of Global Marketing Standardization on Performance," *Journal of Marketing*, 56 (April), 1-17.

Sharma, Subhash, Terence A. Shimp, and Jeongshin Shin (1995), "Consumer Ethnocentrism: A Test of Antecedents and Moderators," *Journal of the Academy of Marketing Science*, 23 (1), 26-37.

Sharma, Subhash, Terence A. Shimp, and Jeongshin Shin (1995), "Consumer Ethnocentrism: A Test of Antecedents and Moderators," *Journal of the Academy of Marketing Science*, 23 (1), 26-37.

Shimp, Terence A. (1984), "Consumer Ethnocentrism: The Concept and A Preliminary Empirical Test," in *Advances in Consumer Research*, Thomas C. Kinnear ed., Vol. XI, Provo, UT: Association for Consumer Research, 285-90.

_____ and Subhash Sharma (1987), "Consumer Ethnocentrism: Construction and Validation of the CETSCALE," *Journal of Marketing Research*, 27 (August), 280-9.

Index

Advertising. *See also* International
   advertising
by services firms, in Hong Kong, 29
Approach-avoidance behavior, 70
Arousal, emotional. *See also*
   Environmental cues, emotional
   influences of
in response to physical environment,
   70-71
Audi, 94
Automobile marketing, 105-106
Automobile servicing, customer service
   satisfaction/switching costs
   relationship in, 5,9-10,12

Bangkok, Thailand, switching costs-
   mediated customer satisfaction
   study in, 7-21
credence properties factors in, 2-4
customer satisfaction/dissatisfaction
   paradigm of, 3
customer satisfaction measurement
   scales for, 8,9-10,21
disconfirmation of expectations
   paradigm of, 4
in experience properties-based
   services, 6-7,12,14
functional performance variables,
   10-11
in high-credence properties services,
   6,12,14
hypothesis of, 7
managerial implications of, 15
moderator regression analysis in,
   8-10,12-13
moderator subgroup analysis in, 8-9

ordinary least squares regression
   analysis in, 8-9
product experience variable, 5
psychological switching costs
   variables, 6-7,14
research methodology of, 7-10,
   20-21
reverse test for heteroscedascity
   in, 9
setup costs variable, 6
switching barriers variable, 5-6
takedown costs variable, 6
technical and performance
   variables, 2-4,10-12,14
Banking services, perceived risk in,
   45
Beauty care services. *See also*
   Hairdressing services
reference group influences on
   informational influences,
   58-59,61
perceived risk analysis of, 59
as privately-consumed luxury
   service, 51-52,55
utilitarian influences, 58-59,
   61-62
value-expressive influences,
   61
Brand decisions, parental influences
   on, 48
Business Guide to Entertainment,
   The, 61
Buying proposal, 90-93,97,102-104

Career management systems,
   Korean, 36